ADDITIONAL PRAISE FOR
MEAN GIRL

"An individualist who built a cult, Ayn Rand aggrandized greed as
a virtue and was the unapologetic purveyor of what Lisa Duggan
brilliantly calls 'optimistic cruelty.' This short, accessible, and
powerful book charts the rise of affective neoliberalism through
the lens of a life. Buy it for anyone who has ever been lured by
The Fountainhead or who needs help shrugging off *Atlas Shrugged*."
Bonnie Honig, author of *Public Things: Democracy in Disrepair*

"With *Mean Girl*, Duggan offers readers a history of how greed and
capitalist accumulation were made cool and sexy. In a historical
moment in which billionaires have been refashioned into
super-beings, her history of this libertarian matriarch provides a
necessary and eye-opening intervention."
Roderick Ferguson, author of *One-Dimensional Queer*

"Reading *Mean Girl* is an exercise in emotional upheaval. One
minute I was laughing out loud, the next crying into my tea, and
then finally feeling confident that human beings cannot allow the
suffocation of Ayn Rand's thinking to get to us. It is a terrific
book only partly about Rand, because it is really an intellectual
history of neoliberalism—and its toxic outcomes."
Vijay Prashad, Director, Tricontinental: Institute for
Social Research

The Publisher and the University of California Press Foundation gratefully acknowledge the generous support of Jamie Rosenthal Wolf, David Wolf, Rick Rosenthal, and Nancy Stephens / The Rosenthal Family Foundation.

Mean Girl

AMERICAN STUDIES NOW:
CRITICAL HISTORIES OF THE PRESENT

Edited by Lisa Duggan and Curtis Marez

Much of the most exciting contemporary work in American Studies refuses the distinction between politics and culture, focusing on historical cultures of power and protest, on the one hand, or the political meanings and consequences of cultural practices, on the other. *American Studies Now* offers concise, accessible, authoritative, e-first books on significant political debates, personalities, and popular cultural phenomena quickly, while such teachable moments are at the forefront of public consciousness.

Mean Girl

Ayn Rand and the Culture of Greed

Lisa Duggan

UNIVERSITY OF CALIFORNIA PRESS

University of California Press, one of the most distin-
guished university presses in the United States, enriches
lives around the world by advancing scholarship in the
humanities, social sciences, and natural sciences. Its
activities are supported by the UC Press Foundation and
by philanthropic contributions from individuals and
institutions. For more information, visit www.ucpress.edu.

University of California Press
Oakland, California

Library of Congress Cataloging-in-Publication Data
Names: Duggan, Lisa, 1954– author.
Title: Mean girl : Ayn Rand and the culture of greed /
    Lisa Duggan.
Description: Oakland, California : University of
    California Press, [2019] | Includes bibliographical
    references. |
Identifiers: LCCN 2018051014 (print) | LCCN 2018054695
    (ebook) | ISBN 9780520967793 (ebook and ePDF) |
    ISBN 9780520294769 (cloth : alk. paper) |
    ISBN 9780520294776 (pbk. : alk. paper)
Subjects: LCSH: Rand, Ayn—Criticism and interpretation. |
    Rand, Ayn—Influence.
Classification: LCC PS3535.A547 (ebook) | LCC PS3535.A547
    Z63 2019 (print) | DDC 813/.52—dc23
LC record available at https://lccn.loc.gov/2018051014

Manufactured in the United States of America

26 25 24 23 22 21 20 19
10 9 8 7 6 5 4 3 2 1

CONTENTS

OVERVIEW

PREFACE

Ayn Rand is the original Mean Girl, an advocate of the kind of ruthless hierarchy at the center of the movie and Broadway musical *Mean Girls*. Her "sense of life," though developed in the early twentieth century, meshes with the age of neoliberal capitalism.

Neoliberal Capitalism · Sense of Life · Structure of Feeling · Cruel Optimism · Optimistic Cruelty

INTRODUCTION. "WHAT IS GOOD FOR ME IS RIGHT"

Ayn Rand's novels featured ruthless "heroes" (initially based on an actual serial killer) and relentlessly advocated capitalism and inequality. But they have also been read in excerpts in the manner of "cult novels" for their feminist and queer elements.

Moral Economy of Inequality · Objectivism · Umberto Eco and Cult Novels · Mary Gaitskill's "Two Girls Fat and Thin" · Ivo van Hove's "The Fountainhead"

CHAPTER 1. "PROUD WOMAN CONQUEROR"

The 1917 Russian revolution led by the Bolsheviks shaped Ayn Rand's antisocialist views for the rest of her life. Her exposure to European and American movies in Petrograd provided a stock of racialized and gendered imperial images that predominated in her fiction. Her novel *We the Living,* set just after the revolution, is her most autobiographical writing.

European "Civilization" · Imperial Russia · The Bolshevik Revolution · "The Mysterious Valley" · "The Indian Tomb" · "We the Living" · European Fascism

CHAPTER 2. "INDIVIDUALISTS OF THE WORLD UNITE!"

Ayn Rand's experience as a scriptwriter in Hollywood in the 1920s shaped her first blockbuster novel, *The Fountainhead.* The procapitalist perspective she developed and expressed in her fiction was based on serious misunderstandings of the workings of commerce, industry, and finance. By the 1940s and 1950s she affiliated with vehement anticommunism as well as with libertarian capitalism.

Hollywood · Cecil B. DeMille · Marriage to Frank O'Connor · "Night of January 16th" · The Individualist Manifesto · "Anthem" · "The Fountainhead" · Isabel Paterson · Wendell Wilkie · House Un-American Activities Committee · Militant Liberalism

CHAPTER 3. "WOULD YOU CUT THE BIBLE?"

The publication of *Atlas Shrugged* and the launching of Objectivism as a movement via the Nathaniel Branden Institute made Ayn Rand a well-known public figure during the 1960s. The novel celebrated the superiority of capitalists and invoked the racialized hierarchies of empire in a sex-saturated romance plot. She was admired by followers but also reviled as a cult leader, and her reputation suffered during the 1970s. Her Objectivist philosophy became one strand in a rising, fractious American right wing.

"Atlas Shrugged" · Nathaniel Branden Institute · Foundation for Economic Education · Volker Fund · Ludwig von Mises · Friedrich Hayek · William F. Buckley and the "National Review" · Murray Rothbard · Whittaker Chambers · Barry Goldwater

CHAPTER 4. "I FOUND A FLAW"

Ayn Rand was a significant figure in the rise of libertarianism and neoliberalism during the 1970s. Libertarianism remained a fringe movement, but neoliberalism came to dominate states and global institutions by the 1980s. Rand was too purist to be a neoliberal, but she helped create the cultural context for everyday neoliberalism—the promotion of selfishness, greed, and inequality. After the 2008 crash, her star rose especially among tech magnates in Silicon Valley. She is admired by many members of the Trump cabinet and many politicians despite significant political differences.

Libertarianism · Neoliberalism · Mont Pelerin Society · Alan Greenspan · Neoliberal Theater of Cruelty · Silicon Valley · Cato Institute · "Reason" Magazine · Donald Trump

PREFACE

As I write in 2018, every news day delivers a fresh jolt. Since the election of President Donald Trump, the questions arise: Is the news surreal, hyperreal, or unreal? How do we grasp the daily spectacle of cultural contempt—for immigrants and minorities, for women, for political dissent, for "losers"? How do we comprehend the level of social and political indifference—toward those who cannot buy security and access to power? How can the U.S. Congress pass a hugely unpopular tax "reform" bill that vastly expands economic inequality? Who *are* these people in power, making these decisions, and what makes them tick?

Mean Girl addresses these questions through a focus on Ayn Rand, the writer whose dour visage presides over the spirit of our time. Author of the hugely popular novels *The Fountainhead* and *Atlas Shrugged,* Rand is the original Mean Girl. Her heroes and heroines prevail over inferior others in ruthless hierarchical worlds not unlike the high school at the center of the 2004 mega-hit movie *Mean Girls,* the quotable bible of millennial meme culture—now also a Broadway musical. The mass popularity of

Mean Girls, which was based on interviews with high school girls conducted by Rosalind Wiseman for her 2002 book *Queen Bees and Wannabes,* reflects the emotional atmosphere of the age of the Plastics (as the most popular girls at fictional North Shore High are called), as well as the era of *Wall Street's* Gordon Gekko, whose motto is "Greed is Good."[1] The culture of greed is the hallmark of the neoliberal era, the period beginning in the 1970s when the protections of the U.S. and European welfare states, and the autonomy of postcolonial states around the world, came under attack. Advocates of neoliberalism worked to reshape global capitalism by freeing transnational corporations from restrictive forms of state regulation, stripping away government efforts to redistribute wealth and provide public services, and emphasizing individual responsibility over social concern. From the 1980s to 2008, neoliberal politics and policies succeeded in expanding inequality around the world. The political climate Ayn Rand celebrated—the reign of brutal capitalism—intensified. Though Ayn Rand's popularity took off in the 1940s, her reputation took a dive during the 1960s and '70s. Then after her death in 1982, during the neoliberal administrations of Ronald Reagan in the United States and Margaret Thatcher in the United Kingdom, her star rose once more. (See chapter 4 for a full discussion of the rise of neoliberalism.)

During the global economic crisis of 2008 it seemed that the neoliberal order might collapse. It lived on, however, in zombie form as discredited political policies and financial practices were restored. But neoliberal capitalism has always been contested, and competing and conflicting political ideas and organizations proliferated and intensified after 2008 as well. Protest politics blossomed on the left with Occupy Wall Street, Black Lives Matter, and opposition to the Dakota Access oil pipeline at the Standing Rock Sioux reservation in the United States, and with the Arab Spring, and other mobilizations around the world. Anti-neoliberal electoral efforts, like the Bernie Sanders campaign for the U.S. presidency, generated excitement as well. But protest and organizing also expanded on the political right, with reactionary populist, racial nationalist, and protofascist gains in such countries as India, the Philippines, Russia, Hungary, and the United States rapidly proliferating. Between these far-right formations on the one side and persistent zombie neoliberalism on the other, operating sometimes at odds and sometimes in cahoots, the Season of Mean is truly upon us.

We are in the midst of a major global, political, economic, social, and cultural transition—but we don't yet know which way we're headed. The incoherence of the Trump administration is symptomatic of the confusion as politicians and business elites jockey with the Breitbart alt-right forces while conservative evangelical Christians pull strings. The unifying threads are meanness and greed, and the spirit of the whole hodgepodge is Ayn Rand.

Rand's ideas are not the key to her influence. Her writing does support the corrosive capitalism at the heart of neoliberalism, though few movers and shakers actually read any of her nonfiction. Her two blockbuster novels, *The Fountainhead* and *Atlas Shrugged,* are at the heart of her incalculable impact. Many politicians and government officials going back decades have cited Rand as a formative influence—particularly finance guru and former Federal Reserve chairman Alan Greenspan, who was a member of Rand's inner circle, and Ronald Reagan, the U.S. president most identified with the national embrace of neoliberal policies. Major figures in business and finance are or have been Rand fans: Jimmy Wales (Wikipedia), Peter Thiel (Paypal), Steve

Jobs (Apple), John Mackey (Whole Foods), Mark Cuban (NBA), John Allison (BB&T Banking Corporation), Travis Kalanik (Uber), Jeff Bezos (Amazon), ad infinitum. There are also large clusters of enthusiasts for Rand's novels in the entertainment industry, from the 1940s to the present—from Barbara Stanwyck, Joan Crawford, and Raquel Welch to Jerry Lewis, Brad Pitt, Angelina Jolie, Rob Lowe, Jim Carrey, Sandra Bullock, Sharon Stone, Ashley Judd, Eva Mendes, and many more. The current Trump administration is stuffed to the gills with Rand acolytes. Trump himself identifies with *Fountainhead* character Howard Roark; former secretary of state Rex Tillerson listed *Atlas Shrugged* as his favorite book in a *Scouting* magazine feature; his replacement Mike Pompeo has been inspired by Rand since his youth. Ayn Rand's influence is ascendant across broad swaths of our dominant political culture—including among public figures who see her as a key to the zeitgeist, without having read a word of her writing.[2]

But beyond the famous or powerful fans, the novels have had a wide popular impact as bestsellers since publication. Along with Rand's nonfiction, they form the core texts for a political/ philosophical movement: Objectivism. There are several U.S.-based Objectivist organizations and innumerable clubs, reading groups, and social circles. A 1991 survey by the Library of Congress and the Book of the Month Club found that only the Bible had influenced readers more than *Atlas Shrugged*, while a 1998 Modern Library poll listed *The Fountainhead* and *Atlas Shrugged* as the two most revered novels in English. *Atlas Shrugged* in particular skyrocketed in popularity in the wake of the 2008 financial crash. The U.S. Tea Party movement, founded in 2009, featured numerous Ayn Rand–based signs and slogans, especially the opening line of *Atlas Shrugged:* "Who is John Galt?" Republican pundit David Frum claimed that the Tea Party was reinventing the GOP as "the party of Ayn Rand." During 2009 as well, sales of *Atlas Shrugged* tripled, and *GQ* magazine called Rand the year's most influential author. A 2010 Zogby poll found that 29 percent of respondents had read *Atlas Shrugged*, and half of those readers said it had affected their political and ethical thinking. In 2018, a business school teacher writing in *Forbes* magazine recommended repeat readings: "Recent events—the bizarro circus that is the 2016 election, the disintegration of Venezuela, and so on make me wonder if a lot of this could have been avoided had we taken *Atlas Shrugged*'s message to heart. It is a book that is worth re-reading every few years."[3] Rand biographer Jennifer Burns asserts simply that Ayn Rand's fiction is "the gateway drug" to right-wing politics in the United States—although her influence extends well beyond the right wing.[4]

But how can the work of this one novelist (also an essayist, playwright, and philosopher), however influential, be a significant source of insight into the rise of a culture of greed? In a word: *sex*. Ayn Rand made acquisitive capitalists sexy. She launched thousands of teenage libidos into the world of reactionary politics on a wave of quivering excitement. This sexiness extends beyond romance to infuse the creative aspirations, inventiveness, and determination of her heroes with erotic energy, embedded in what Rand called her "sense of life." Analogous to what Raymond Williams has called a "structure of feeling," Rand's *sense of life* combines the libido-infused desire for heroic individual achievement with contempt for social inferiors and indifference to their plight.[5] Lauren Berlant has called the structure of feeling, or emotional situation, of those who struggle for a good life under neoliberal conditions "cruel optimism"—the complex of feelings necessary to keep plugging away hopefully despite setbacks and losses.[6] Rand's contrasting sense of life applies to those whose fantasies of success and domination include no doubt or guilt. The feelings of aspiration and glee that enliven Rand's novels combine with contempt for and indifference to others. The resulting Randian sense of life might be called "optimistic cruelty." Optimistic cruelty is the sense of life for the age of greed.

Ayn Rand's optimistic cruelty appeals broadly and deeply through its circulation of familiar narratives: the story of "civilizational" progress, the belief in American exceptionalism, and a commitment to capitalist freedom. Her novels engage fantasies of European imperial domination conceived as technological and cultural advancement, rather than as violent conquest. America is imagined as a clean slate for pure capitalist freedom, with no indigenous people, no slaves, no exploited immigrants or workers in sight. *The Fountainhead* and especially *Atlas Shrugged* fabricate history and romanticize violence and domination in ways that reflect, reshape, and reproduce narratives of European superiority and American virtue. Their logic also depends on a hierarchy of value based on racialized beauty and physical capacity—perceived ugliness or disability are equated with pronounced worthlessness and incompetence. Through the forms of romance and melodrama, Rand novels extrapolate the story of racial capitalism as a story of righteous passion and noble virtue. They retell *The Birth of a Nation* through the lens of industrial capitalism (see chapter 2). They solicit positive identification with winners, with dominant historical forces. It is not an accident that the novels' fans, though gender mixed, are overwhelmingly white Americans of the professional, managerial, creative, and business classes.[7] Ayn Rand's identification with dominance was not seamless, however. As a Russian Jewish woman, her experiences of ethnic/religious and gender inequality gave her fiction's sense of life some important kinks, some twists and turns. These kinks attracted readers from a range of viewpoints, not all unalloyed procapitalist zealots.

Mean Girl traces the development of Rand's writing from her life in revolutionary Russia to her arrival in Hollywood and her love for New York City, over the course of her morphing political commitments to the antisocialist politics that infused her life's work. Its chapters examine the impact and influence of her writing to ask: Where are we now? Is the long career of optimistic cruelty, of contempt and indifference to human inequality, at its height? Or is the culture of greed surrounding zombie neoliberalism so pronounced now that it is effectively exposed and may finally be displaced as an acceptable political feeling? Cultural critic Slavoj Žižek has argued that Rand's mad adoration of capitalism, her excessive overidentification with it, only serves to make its inherent ridiculousness clearly perceptible.[8]

Mean Girl grapples with these questions. It is not a biography of Rand. Nor is it social history based in original archival research, or literary criticism based in close readings of key texts. It belongs to American cultural studies, grasped through a global frame. It is focused on illuminating the "how did we get here?" questions, via analysis and speculation about the role of feeling, fantasy, and desire in constructing and maintaining political economies.

Introduction

"What Is Good for Me Is Right"

It usually begins with Ayn Rand.

The young crusader in search of a cause enters the world of *The Fountainhead* or *Atlas Shrugged* as though he were about to engage in unheard-of-sexual delights for the first time. He has been warned beforehand. There is no need to search any further. The quest is over. Here is all the truth you've been looking for contained in the tightly packed pages of two gargantuan novels.

Jerome Tuccille, *It Usually Begins with Ayn Rand,* 1971[1]

Before we get to the sexual delights, we must begin with murder.

William Edward Hickman was a forger, armed robber, kidnapper, and multiple murderer. In 1927, at the age of nineteen, he appeared at a Los Angeles public school and lured twelve-year-old Marion Parker into accompanying him, supposedly to visit her father, hospitalized after a car accident. Over the next few days he sent her parents a series of taunting ransom notes. Marion's father collected the ransom money and delivered it to Hickman. As he delivered the cash he could see his daughter in the passenger seat of Hickman's car as he drove off, only to dump her body at the end of the street. The killer had dismembered her body, drained it of blood, cut her internal organs out, and stuffed her torso with bath towels. He had wired her eyes open to make her seem alive and propped her body upright in his car, swathed in clothing. Pieces of her body were found all over LA.[2]

In her journal, the young Ayn Rand began outlining the character of the imagined hero of her first planned (but never completed) novel in English, titled *The Little Street*. Her hero, a nineteen-year-old boy she named Danny Renahan, was based on William Hickman. Rand composed a long paragraph listing all the things she liked about Hickman: "The fact that he looks like a bad boy with a very winning grin, that he makes you like him the whole time you're in his presence." She confessed her "involuntary, irresistible sympathy for him, which I cannot help feeling...in spite of everything." About the slogan he announced at trial, "I am like the state: what is good for me is right," Rand wrote, "Even if he wasn't big enough to live by that attitude, he deserves credit for saying it so brilliantly."[3]

Rand noted that Renahan was not simply a copy of Hickman: "It is more exact to say that the model is not Hickman, but what Hickman suggested to me." She drew from Hickman's "wonderful 'sense of living'" and his "brazenly challenging attitude," which can be seen in

> his utter remorselessness, his pride in his criminal career and in things that are considered a "disgrace"; his boasting of more and more crimes and his open joy at shocking people, instead of trying to implore their sympathy; his utter lack of anything that is considered a "virtue"; his strength as shown in his unprecedented conduct during his trial and sentencing; his *calm, superior, indifferent, disdainful countenance* [emphasis added], which is like an open challenge to

society—shouting to it that it cannot break him; his immense explicit egotism—a thing the mob never forgives; and his *cleverness,* which makes the mob feel that a superior mind can exist entirely outside its established morals. (emphasis added)

Renahan was not the only notoriously antisocial figure to serve as a model for Rand's fiction. Her 1934 play *Night of January 16th* (premiered as *Woman on Trial* at the Hollywood Playhouse) was based on the career and possible 1932 murder of Swedish financier and notorious swindler Ivar Kreuger, whom John Kenneth Galbraith named the "Leonardo of larcenists."[4] Later in her career Rand made it quite clear that she did not admire their crimes; what she admired was certain criminals who were hounded by "the mob" for their exceptional qualities.

In her notes on *The Little Street,* Rand compared Hickman/ Renahan to a Nietzschean "Superman." Although her journals are replete with such superficial vulgarizations of Nietzsche (whom she later repudiated), the "Superman" she references may have more in common with the comic book character invented a few years later, in 1933. As popular economics writer Michael Goodwin notes, Ayn Rand's books, "like Superman comics[,] are fantasies," and "fantasies are powerful."[5]

Beginning with Danny Renahan, Rand started work on her most powerful fantasy, the profile for the heroes who would appear in future novels, with their starkly stylized "sense of life." In *The Romantic Manifesto* (1969) she explained that "the motive and purpose of my writing is the projection of an ideal man ... *as an end in himself*—not as a means to any further end."[6] Her ideal man morphs from novel to novel, carrying with him the core characteristics of passionate creativity and an unconflicted sense of superiority. He showcases contempt for lesser beings and cool indifference to their suffering—even to their very existence. He is guiltless. He can be recognized by his strongly masculine physical beauty, manner, and gait. His sexual magnetism is tied to his surly, casual cruelty. His special, enabling skill is his ability to alienate himself from the people around him. He is her fantasy consort, her leading man, the Mean Boy who goes beyond contempt for and indifference to weak, inferior others. He conveys, like William Hickman, an erotic investment in death and destruction. He is the avatar for optimistic cruelty.

There is of course nothing original in this profile. Rand's ideal man shares many key characteristics with the heroes of romantic fiction and adventure tales, from nineteenth-century melodramas to twenty-first-century romance novels. Rand determinedly appropriated a version of this romantic hero from European graphic fiction that she read as a child. She incorporated the fantasy figures of European empire that she found there—domineering, manly adventurers and conquistadors—into her own defenses of nineteenth- and twentieth-century individualist capitalism.[7]

It is sorely tempting to ridicule Ayn Rand's work, her cartoonish characters and melodramatic plots, her rigid moralizing, her middle- to lowbrow aesthetic preferences (she preferred Rachmaninoff to Beethoven, Mickey Spillane to Eugene O'Neill) and philosophical strivings. It is difficult to resist rather crudely psychoanalyzing or otherwise diagnosing her, explaining her body of work as the compensatory fantasy life of a tortured soul who was perhaps a sociopath, but at least a malignant narcissist. It is nearly inevitable that those who do not become fans are appalled by Rand's celebration of cruelty and inequality. But these responses will not help us understand the enormous impact of Ayn Rand's oeuvre. If we are interested in careful expositions of Milton Friedman's economic theories, and in historical analyses of the operations of the International Monetary Fund—both crucial to the rise and spread of neoliberal capitalism—then we should be pressed into serious consideration of the work of Ayn Rand. Her influence on the world that neoliberalism made has been profound. Engaging her writing rather than dismissing it is crucial to grasping where we are now.

It might be objected that Ayn Rand's ideas—expressed in her fiction and philosophy—are too crude and derivative to matter. But Rand's core contributions to neoliberal political culture do not consist of ideas. Rand's novels, especially, are conversion machines that run on lust. They create feelings of aspiration and desire in readers, who often encounter *The Fountainhead* or *Atlas Shrugged* in high school. They feed fantasies of the Good Life, a future of adventure and achievement against all odds. They engender a Randian sense of life that leads many readers (though certainly not all) into conservative or right-wing politics with the passion and energy of a convert, of a true believer. They provide a structure of feeling—optimistic cruelty—that morphs throughout the twentieth century and underwrites the form of capitalism on steroids that dominates the present.[8]

Ayn Rand defines her "sense of life" as "a pre-conceptual equivalent of metaphysics, an emotional, subconsciously integrated appraisal of man and of existence. It sets the nature of a man's emotional responses and the essence of his character."[9] This sense of life underlies the eventual rational integration of a philosophy of living; reason and emotion are fully, seamlessly integrated in the properly functioning Randian man and woman. Their sense of life is individual and ahistorical. But if we reinterpret Rand's sense of life through Raymond Williams's structure of feeling (see preface), we can find a way to historicize her representations of emotional life. Williams describes "social experiences in solution" as markers of living processes that are widely perceived.[10] This view helps us see Rand's sense of life as a concentrated, individualized representation of historical experience. The wide appeal of her fiction confirms that her sense of life resonates within a social context. Following Lauren Berlant's gloss on Williams, we might see Rand's sense of life as like Berlant's *affect*, registering "the conditions of life that move across persons and worlds, play out in lived time, and energize attachments."[11]

Ayn Rand's person and world began in 1905 in St. Petersburg, where she was born with the name Alissa Rosenbaum. Along with many other secular urban Jews in the turn-of-the-century Russian empire, she grew to identify strongly with European imperial centers. This devotion to European "civilization" was complicated for the daughter of Russian Jews in a male-dominated, anti-Semitic context. Her profound ambivalence toward Jewish and female subjects deeply marked her entire professional career and private life. During the 1917 Bolshevik revolution her father's pharmacy was seized, and the family never recovered their relatively privileged social and economic position. This dispossession was formative for Alissa Rosenbaum, generating a lifelong feeling of outraged entitlement flowing from her belief that the life she deserved had been stolen from her. It also shaped her decision to migrate to the United States in 1926. She made her way to Hollywood, where she changed her name to Ayn Rand, worked as a junior script writer for Cecil B. DeMille, and began to both elaborate and live her fantasies—in film scripts, novels, and plays, and in her marriage to handsome film extra Frank O'Connor. She transferred her dreams of guiltless empire and glittering capitalism from Europe to the U.S., moving to New York in 1951 to build the philosophical movement called Objectivism.

But life was not exactly a dream for Ayn Rand. Although she did publish a series of novels and a play—*We the Living* (1936), *Night of January 16th* (1936), *Anthem* (1938), *The Fountainhead* (1943), and *Atlas Shrugged* (1957)—and her writing was increasingly successful over time, attracting a devoted following, there were also years of bitter struggle, sharply critical reviews, and elite opprobrium, followed by depression and self-medication with benzedrine. Objectivism was riven with conflict and often identified by critics as a cult. The group nearly dissolved in 1968 in the wake of her bitter split with a younger acolyte with whom she had a secret affair. The handsome husband she touted as her real-life hero, described by friends as a sweet and passive man who loved flowers and peacocks, deteriorated and died of alcoholism and despair.

In the 1960s and '70s, Rand abandoned fiction writing and put out a series of collections of excerpts, essays, and polemics outlining the philosophy of Objectivism and her goals as a thinker and writer: *For the New Intellectual* (1961), *The Virtue of Selfishness* (1964), *Capitalism: The Unknown Ideal* (1966), *The Romantic Manifesto* (1969), *The New Left: The Anti-Industrial Revolution* (1971), and *Introduction to Objectivist Epistemology* (1979). Many of the essays and segments in these collections were originally published in the *Objectivist Newsletter,* later to become the *Objectivist,* a magazine. Taken together, these publications constituted a kind of footnote to her fiction; she regarded *Atlas Shrugged* as her signal achievement and the prime expression of her views.

Also during the 1960s and '70s, Ayn Rand became a recognizable figure on campuses, in popular culture, and in conflict-ridden libertarian political circles. She lectured widely, scored a *Playboy* interview with futurist Alvin Toffler in 1964, appeared on television interviewed by Mike Wallace in 1959 and by Johnny Carson in 1967. In 1974, she was photographed with disciple Alan

Greenspan and President Gerald Ford in the Oval Office, during Greenspan's swearing in as chairman of Ford's Council of Economic Advisors. The *Playboy* editors provided a respectful but pointed introduction to her interview that outlines Rand's contradictory reputation at the time:

> Ayn Rand, an intense, angry young woman of 58, is among the most outspoken—and important—intellectual voices in America today. She is the author of what is perhaps the most fiercely damned and admired best seller of the decade: *Atlas Shrugged*, which has sold 1,200,000 copies since its publication six years ago, and has become one of the most talked-about novels in the country. Ayn Rand discussion clubs dot college campuses. Professors debate her ideas in their classrooms. More than 2,500 people in 30 cities from New York to Los Angeles attend courses given by the Nathaniel Branden Institute, in which they listen to live speakers and taped lectures expounding the principles set forth in the book. Thousands more subscribe to *The Objectivist Newsletter,* a monthly publication in which Miss Rand and her associates comment on everything from economics to aesthetics. And sales of her previous best seller, *The Fountainhead,* have climbed to almost the 2,000,000 mark. That any novel should set off such a chain reaction is unusual; that *Atlas Shrugged* has done so is astonishing. For the book, a panoramic novel about what happens when the "men of the mind" go on strike, is 1168 pages long. It is filled with lengthy, sometimes complex philosophical passages; and it is brimming with as many explosively unpopular ideas as Ayn Rand herself. Despite this success, the literary establishment considers her an outsider. Almost to a man, critics have either ignored or denounced the book. She is an exile among philosophers, too, although *Atlas* is as much a work of philosophy as it is a novel. Liberals glower at the very mention of her name; but conservatives, too, swallow hard when she begins to speak. For Ayn Rand, whether anyone likes it or not, is sui generis: indubitably, irrevocably, intransigently individual. She detests the drift of modern American society. She doesn't like its politics, its

economics, its attitudes toward sex, women, business, art or religion. In short, she declares with unblinking immodesty, "I am challenging the cultural tradition of two-and-a-half-thousand years." She means it....

... Miss Rand spoke clearly and urgently about her work and her views. Answering question after question with a clipped, even delivery, her deep voice edged with a Russian accent, she paused only long enough between words to puff on a cigarette held in a blue-and-silver holder (a gift from admirers) engraved with her initials, the names of the three heroes of *Atlas Shrugged*, and a number of diminutive dollar signs. The dollar sign, in *Atlas Shrugged*, is the symbol of "free trade and, therefore, of a free mind."[12]

Rand's complicated notoriety as popular writer, leader of a political/philosophical cult, reviled intellectual, and kitschy public figure (often posed in photos with a cape and huge dollar-sign pin as well as cigarette holder) followed her past her death in 1982. But she has been resurrected in the twenty-first century as a seriously regarded reference point for mainstream figures, especially (but not only) those on the political right. She is reborn and ubiquitous in the neoliberal pantheon especially.

Ayn Rand's integrated philosophy is not the basis for this resurgence of political and cultural influence; her ideas matter primarily as the framework for her fictional universe. Her Objectivist philosophy is starkly basic enough that she easily summarized it for a Random House salesman who asked her to present the essence of her views while standing on one foot. According to Rand, "I did as follows: 1) Metaphysics: Objective Reality; 2) Epistemology: Reason; 3) Ethics: Self-interest; 4) Politics: Capitalism." She elaborated by asserting that reality exists as an objective absolute (she credits this to Aristotle), reason is the only means of perceiving reality and acquiring knowledge, every man is an end in himself, and the ideal political-economic system is laissez-faire capitalism.[13] These ideas took shape initially as anti-Bolshevism, then expanded into the basis for her bitter opposition to the welfare state. They then energized the postwar anti-communist commitment that motivated her to testify eagerly before the House Un-American Activities Committee in 1947. All along the way Rand drew on the defenses of empire, capitalism, and inequality around her—including civilizational discourses, possessive individualism, and social Darwinism. She claimed status as an Aristotelian philosopher of the first rank, but only her most devoted followers shared that view. Her particular gift was not for philosophical elaboration, but for stark condensation and aphorism. She deployed this gift to create a *moral economy of inequality* to infuse her softly pornographic romance fiction with the political eros that would captivate a mass readership.

Rand's alignment with neoliberal thinking began in the 1940s and '50s. Ludwig von Mises, the prominent Austrian School economist and founder of the neoliberal Mont Pelerin Society, admired *Atlas Shrugged*. He wrote to Rand in 1958 to invite her to attend his seminar at New York University as an honored guest and commented, "You have the courage to tell the masses what no politician told them: you are inferior and all the improvements in your conditions which you simply take for granted you owe to the effort of men who are better than you."[14]

Rand's posthumous appeal has not been limited to the fractious overlapping company of neoliberals, libertarians, conservatives, and right-wing politicians, however. Voluminous commentary testifies to the appeal of Rand's novels to adolescents who grow into adults with a wide variety of political commitments. Mimi Gladstein's anthology *Feminist Interpretations of Ayn Rand* collects a stunning array of feminist responses to Rand's novels, from enthusiasm (Billie Jean King) or revulsion (Susan

Brownmiller) to the camp appropriations outlined by Melanie Jane Hardie in "Fluff and Granite: Rereading Ayn Rand's Camp Aesthetics."[15] Mary Gaitskill's 1991 feminist novel *Two Girls, Fat and Thin*, bases the character of Anna Granite (founder of Definitism) on Rand. The Definitist follower and the journalist who are the central characters (the "two girls") are shaped by Gaitskill's interviews with Rand disciples. Her characterizations are at once nuanced and sympathetic overall, yet critical to the point of hilarious parody at moments.[16]

Despite Rand's widely known description of homosexuality as "immoral" and "disgusting," her complex influence is also reflected in LGBT and queer commentary on Rand. The novelist's libertarian rages against the strictures of family, church, and state appeal to many LGBTQ readers, many of whom also enjoy searching for unconventional sexual arrangements and homoerotic exchanges between characters. In his online blog post "Queer Themes in Ayn Rand," Gabriel Mitchell delightedly notes that "non-monogamy is prevalent in both of her major novels.... [Dagny Taggart in *Atlas Shrugged* finds herself] passionately loving multiple partners without concern for labels or exclusivity.... Homoerotic tension is also ripe between the male heroes."[17] Queer fans go on to make varying investments in Rand's broader political or philosophical framework.[18]

Prominent Belgian theater director and self-identified gay social democrat Ivo van Hove fell in love with *The Fountainhead* when he received it as a gift in 2007. He wrote and directed a four-hour play based on it that debuted in 2014 to excellent reviews. Neither a parody nor simply a dramatic cartoon, van Hove's production emphasizes the struggle of a creative artist, architect Howard Roark, against the forces of conventionality and mediocrity.[19] This kind of focused, selective emphasis is available to all interpreters of novels for the stage (or film). But Rand's novels are particularly prone to reading in the manner of "cult novels" as described by Umberto Eco, with sections or isolated themes excerpted as the text is broken apart by readers for divergent purposes.[20] Even the readers most loyal to Rand's overall political vision often fiercely advocate some of her views while ignoring others—especially her atheism.

The particular alchemy of influence varies widely among readers, fans, and followers, but Rand's novels nonetheless operate primarily as conversion machines for our contemporary culture of greed. The following chapters of *Mean Girl* trace that work from the Russian revolution through some of the major social conflicts of the twentieth century to the dilemmas we face in the political present.

ONE

"Proud Woman Conqueror"

Socialist revolution made Ayn Rand. Her key ideas and primary narrative strategies acquired shape and energy as the Bolsheviks took St. Petersburg in 1917. Her childhood idealization of the values and achievements of European "civilization" merged with furious antisocialism in that vortex. Her earliest fiction—the movie script "Red Pawn" and her first novel, *We the Living*—drew heavily on her life in Russia for images, feelings, and narrative arcs. She imagined her first heroes and conjured the "mobs" that threatened them in the years before she left for the United States in 1926, at the age of twenty-one.

Alissa Zinovievna Rosenbaum was born in the heart of the late Russian empire in 1905. The prosperous Rosenbaums were among the very small number of Jewish families permitted residence in the imperial capital of St. Petersburg. Alissa's father, Zelman Wolf Zakharovich Rosenbaum (called Zinovy), had been born in the Pale of Settlement, the area where most Jews were required to live. Despite quotas for Jewish students in higher education, he trained as a pharmaceutical chemist at the

University of Warsaw and thereby earned the right to move to St. Petersburg. His wife, Khana Berkovna Kaplan (called Anna), was a dentist who belonged to the Jewish elite of that city. Her tailor father owned a factory in St. Petersburg that made military uniforms for the tsar's guards, a position that provided an exemption to the anti-Semitic residency restrictions. Zinovy worked among his in-laws, advancing to ownership of a pharmacy by 1917. Anna gave up her dental practice after marriage and raised three daughters. As the family prospered they moved to fashionable Nevsky Prospekt, where they employed servants, tutored their three daughters in French and music, summered abroad, and sent Alissa (the eldest) to a school for privileged young ladies that had evaded the usual severe restrictions on Jewish enrollment. Alissa made one friend there—Olga Nabokov, Vladimir's sister.[1]

It was in this world that Alissa began to imagine herself as a writer. By her teenage years, she was deeply immersed in reading and writing fiction. She developed her first romantic fixation in 1914, on the leading character of a serial adventure story in a French children's magazine: Cyrus Paltons, the hero of "The Mysterious Valley." The story, set in British-ruled India in 1911, features a captivating British infantry captain. Colonial adventures abound, rife with exoticized natives. Paltons is carried by trained Bengali tigers to a hidden valley, occupied by (of course) bloodthirsty Hindu shamans. A team of rescuers led by a French archeologist arrives, and all are ultimately led out of the valley by Cyrus. Looking back from above after their escape, they watch fires and a flood wipe out the Hindu inhabitants.

This Orientalist scenario (strongly echoed in parts of Rand's last novel, *Atlas Shrugged*) was a children's-cartoonish version of commonplace European imperial fantasies. Alissa Rosenbaum's fixation on Paltons reflected her idealization of the British (to be replaced later by Americans) as models of imperial conquest. Cyrus was handsome, tall, arrogant, and romantically involved with a beautiful British woman. He represented "civilization" to Alissa, embodying the conquering values of the highest type of man. His superiority was reflected in his physical type as much as in his domineering attitude and actions. Her hero! Long before her crush on William Hickman, this heroic figure was defined by violence. The Hindus in the valley constitute a template for the "mob" that must be defeated or destroyed for the heroes of civilization to triumph. Their fate illuminates the racial domination and genocide that are the ground for civilizational achievement. This kind of "mob" appears throughout Alissa/Ayn's fiction.[2]

Strong identification with European "civilization" (including the British) was pervasive in Alissa Rosenbaum's milieu. Her own identification with Western modernity was complicated by ambivalence generated specifically through her Jewishness and her position as an educated urban girl. Among the urban Jewish elite, secular assimilationist aspirations ruled, and disidentification with Jewishness was not unusual. Nonetheless, the pervasive restrictions and regulations and periodic anti-Semitic violence strengthened bonds of community forged in resistance to widespread danger and hostility. Even where religious identification flagged, a kind of cultural affinity persisted, however unevenly.

Alissa Rosenbaum strongly disidentified with Judaism, calling herself an atheist by age thirteen. She chose heroes and models who were radically unlike the people around her—tall, often blond, muscular Aryan physical types. But as she aspired to reach beyond exclusion and victimization to join the conquering heroes, there were some chinks in her acquired armor. She dimly recognized herself in some angry outsiders, and unselfconsciously surrounded herself with a critical mass of secular Jewish intellectuals throughout her life. This ambivalence shaped her worldview in myriad ways, inflecting her love of domineering conquerors with an integral rage and hatred that sometimes aimed up as well as down the hierarchies she celebrated.[3]

It is *not* fair or accurate to say that Ayn Rand's politics were somehow Jewish. A disproportionate number of the Bolshevik leaders she despised and opposed were also Jewish. Jews are a widely diverse and divergent group, scattered across nearly every ideological spectrum. But not in a purely random way. As with other excluded or oppressed groups, the experience of marginalization does not determine political views, but it does shape the forms they take and leaves traces in the affective tenor of political commitments. Rand's experience of anti-Semitism gave her work a critical edge. Her angry response to complacent entitlement allowed her work to appeal to outsiders (including feminists and queers), though she herself could be quite anti-Semitic. The experience of anti-Semitism shaped how Jews participated in politics across the whole political spectrum, from communism to capitalism. As Rand's views evolved over the twentieth century, eventually reaching vast audiences through her novels, a complex and contradictory foundation for her appeal emerged.[4]

In addition to her position as a prosperous secular urban Jewish subject of the late Russian empire, Alissa Rosenbaum struggled with the predicament of being female. On the one hand, many educated urbanites in late imperial Russia supported women's careers and political involvements. A minority of libertarian radicals, influenced by nineteenth-century utopian thinking, supported "free love" over marriage and advocated economic independence and reproductive autonomy (birth control and abortion on demand) for women. But these progressively "modern" beliefs existed alongside traditional familialism and powerful misogyny. The challenges of living as a "modern" woman, torn between new opportunities and persisting responsibilities for home and children, vexed every progressive social group across the spectrum of liberal to left political formations. Alissa Rosenbaum had a very hard time working out a way to live with those contradictions. She pushed hard against familialism toward aspirational modernity, while contending with highly gendered imperial ideals of beauty, strength, and virtue—ideals she both reproduced and contested. From a very young age she wanted to be a writer and devote her life to her art! But she also wanted to create conventionally beautiful, seductive romantic heroines, recognizably feminine to readers and irresistible to the heroes.

Alissa's first image of heroic femininity was Daisy, a British girl she saw playing tennis. Daisy appeared to her as an apparition—beautiful, athletic, living a carefree life. Later in London the apparition recurred in the form of a theatrical poster featuring girls like Daisy, with modern English pageboy haircuts. Alissa remembered these sightings as the inspiration for her decision to become a writer. Her first template for a heroine invoked a fantasy of feminine glamour, imbued with the confidence that accompanied imperial and class privilege.[5]

Meanwhile back in St. Petersburg the Bolsheviks seized power. Nothing was ever the same after that. Not for Alissa Rosenbaum and not for the world. A new possibility appeared on the horizon of the twentieth century: the possibility of a worker/peasant alliance seizing state power under the direction of a vanguard party. This possibility was enthralling and exhilarating, or nightmarish and terrifying for counterrevolutionaries. In either case it was a world historical turning point.

Alissa Rosenbaum had lived her short life oblivious to the existence of workers and peasants except as shadowy apparitions, specters of irrationality, or properly subordinated social inferiors. Then oh my god: there they were in the Winter Palace and at her door, behaving as equals and asserting their collective will with the backing of state power. In the midst of food and housing shortages, her family lost their privileged access to resources. The family home was seized and her father's pharmacy was nationalized. She had no framework for understanding what was happening other than the raw experience of loss. She was not aware of the injustices that motivated the Bolsheviks or the workers and peasants who supported them. She had no access to their aspirations, fantasies, and desires. All Alissa saw was resentment, envy, theft, bullying, and the exercise of illegitimate power by people who did not deserve it and could not exercise it rationally. She rewrote the vast canvas of social, economic, and political conflict underlying the Bolshevik revolution—between Russians and non-Russians, poor peasants and landowning kulaks, workers and bosses, nationalists and internationalists, Christians and Muslims, Marxists and populists—into a stark melodramatic clash between worthy individuals and the mob. Not a surprising reductive analysis for a sheltered and privileged twelve-year-old caught in the swirl of overwhelming events. But she stuck to it and elaborated it for the rest of her life.[6]

The Rosenbaums left St. Petersburg (now called Petrograd) for the Crimea, hoping the whole thing would blow over. It didn't. They returned to Petrograd to live in a small part of their now divided former home, and to struggle for the limited available supply of food and fuel. The Bolsheviks' New Economic Policy (NEP, 1921–1928) addressed economic devastation with a loosening of restrictions on private trade. Zinovy Rosenbaum reopened his pharmacy (though it was soon closed again), and Alissa went to college, now tuition free and open to women and

Jews. She concentrated in history and fell in love with a young Jewish man, Lev Bekkerman—her first living romantic interest. In a later interview, Ayn Rand remembered:

> The first time I saw him I remember being very startled by how good-looking he was. He entered the room and I couldn't quite believe it. He didn't look quite real in the sense that he was too perfectly good looking.... What was unusual is that he was my type of face, with one exception, he had dark hair rather than light hair. But he had light gray eyes, and was tall.... Very intelligent face, very determined ... self-confidant. And the quality that I liked about him most was arrogance.... But ... not boastful, not vanity, but actually what he projected was pride, with a kind of haughty smile.... There was always a smile behind his attitude, and an arrogant smile of, "Well, world, you have to admire me." That sort of attitude ... like some fantastic aristocrat.[7]

Lev Bekkerman became the model for Leo Kovalensky, the hero of her first published novel, *We the Living.*

In the midst of the struggle for necessities and the demands of school, Alissa hoarded money and made time for cultural diversions that both entertained her and gave form to her developing imagination. Her tastes ran to middlebrow and popular entertainments, rather than to European high culture or the emerging Soviet avant-garde. Mostly, she loved the movies.

Foreign-made films rolled into cities of the Russian empire during the early twentieth century, with a fledgling native industry established in Moscow by 1907–1908. The industry grew, with American films slowly replacing French and German productions. Films on offer included newsreels, historical dramas, serials, adaptations of classic novels, genre pictures, and contemporary melodramas. Overall the movies created a public venue that especially attracted the professional and merchant classes while also generating cross-class appeal (though individual theaters tended to be class differentiated).[8]

During the NEP period, the Bolshevik government supported the film industry. As signs and banners around the theaters in Petrograd proclaimed, "Comrade Lenin Said: Of all the arts, the most important one for Russia is the cinema!" Alissa Rosenbaum enrolled in the State Institute for Cinematography in 1924 to learn screenwriting. She attended more than 150 movies and kept a movie diary. Her favorite was a 1921 German imperial melodrama, *The Indian Tomb,* which starred movie idol (and Alissa's first ranked male star) Conrad Veidt. This Orientalist fantasy shared thematic elements with Alissa's beloved magazine adventure story "The Mysterious Valley." A maharajah commissions an English architect to build a shrine more impressive than the Taj. But upon arrival the architect discovers that the shrine is to be a living-death tomb for the maharajah's unfaithful lover. The film is replete with elephants, palaces, tigers, lascivious queens, and exotic smoky clubs. The lover kills herself, the architect escapes with his white fiancé. All the major Indian roles are played by Germans in blackface.[9]

Young Alissa's love of this film, like her love for Cyrus Paltons, made its way into her fiction. The physical descriptions, the characterizations, the thrill of conquest, the eroticization of dominant masculinity, the figures of the hero and the mob, can be traced to the representations of romanticized imperialism all around her.

While enrolled at the cinematography school, Alissa began to write for publication. The pamphlet "Hollywood: American City of Movies" was probably written as a class assignment, then edited and published without her knowledge or permission in 1926.[10] Her mother found it in a bookstore after Alissa left Russia.

Consisting primarily of breathless, amazed, gushing descriptions of the Stars! the Studios! the Money!, the pamphlet demonstrates a fairly extensive knowledge of Hollywood personalities gathered from the movie magazines sent by relatives in Chicago. Her descriptions expound her view from afar of (for her) a thrilling kind of Hollywood globalism:

> The movies they produce seize every country, each nation. Just as you will find scenery depicting any part of the world around Hollywood, so on its streets you will meet representatives of every nationality, people from every social class. Elegant Europeans, energetic, businesslike Americans, benevolent Negroes, quiet Chinese, savages from colonies, Professors from the best schools, farmers, and aristocrats of all types and ages descend on the Hollywood studios in a greedy crowd.

This pamphlet marks the beginning of the transfer of Alissa's imperial fantasies, with everyone in their assigned place on the scale of civilizational "progress," from the European to the American context. Notably, the pamphlet does not mention the presence of any Jewish people in Hollywood.

Alissa's second pamphlet, a paean to Polish movie star Pola Negri, also marked that transfer.[11] Negri was the first European film star to be invited to Hollywood. She became one of the most popular actresses in American silent movies, whose love affairs with Rudolph Valentino and others were closely followed in the movie magazines. The profile of Negri veers away from Alissa's childhood idealizations of sunny blonde English girls. She describes Negri as a "gloomy, intense, cruel woman" with "dark tragic eyes" that narrow in a "wearily derisive way." A "proud woman conqueror" if often also "tragic," Negri in Hollywood is "the only human being among mannequins." Not one of the "fragile virtuous maidens" of sentimental American drama, Negri had a "joyless" childhood and an unhappy private life as an adult. She was, Alissa wrote, "unattractive" but nonetheless desired for her uniqueness. She is redeemed and exalted by her utter devotion to her art, above all else.

This may not have been an especially good description of Negri, but it was a fairly revealing, if projected, self-perception. Laced through this deeply ambivalent description, a critique of the expectations of femininity emerges. Here was a famous movie star, glamorous and desired, who was darkly moody, unsmiling, unhappy, even angry in that derisively contemptuous way that Alissa revered. She was, in Alissa's imagination, indifferent to the opinions of others yet widely adored. The sense of outsiderness that Alissa located in Negri, the conviction of not being like the other "empty mannequins" and "virtuous maidens," generates strength and specialness. Negri, in this profile, stands as a conquering Americanized European, superior without the sunny complacent entitlement, glamorously feminine without the deferential niceness. Here was an ambivalent tangle of qualities and affects that could appeal to the conflicted aspirations of Alissa Rosenbaum, a young Russian Jewish woman, and to so many others.

Alissa yearned to go to the United States to work as a screenwriter and become a novelist. With her rather uncanny ability to get what she wanted, she beat the considerable odds and got out of Soviet Russia in 1926. With the pooled resources of her economically strapped family, she made her way to New York, Chicago, and Hollywood. She started work on *We the Living* in 1929 but took a break to earn some money by writing a script for a movie original, also set in Soviet Russia. "Red Pawn" was considered by Josef von Sternberg as a vehicle for Marlene Dietrich, but it was never produced.[12]

Rand described *We the Living,* published in 1936, as closer to an autobiography than any of her other writing.[13] The novel begins with the heroine, Kira Argounova (the character based on Rand), traveling from the Crimea back to her home in Petrograd with her family in 1922. The initial focus is on the gritty details of moving into the family apartment, now shared, and searching for work, food, and fuel in conditions of poverty and scarcity following years of war. Encounters with petty Bolshevik bureaucrats and scheming private traders during the NEP years are detailed for outrage or humor. The plot then follows Kira to college, where she studies engineering. She attends endless meetings with finagling, ambitious students, and encounters the first purges of university students (Rand herself was purged then reinstated while a student at Petrograd State University).

Rand then introduces the other two central characters, Andrei Taganov and Leo Kovalensky. Andrei is a Party member who stands out by virtue of his integrity. Leo is a former aristocrat, on the run and in all kinds of trouble. Both fall in love with Kira, though she only truly loves Leo. The plot picks up steam when Leo is diagnosed with tuberculosis but barred from the state sanitariums by virtue of his lineage. In order to raise the money for a private sanitarium in the Crimea, Kira tumbles into bed with Andrei—who believes he is giving her money to help her family. Kira tells Leo that the money comes from a relative living abroad.

The triangle explodes when Leo returns to Kira cured. Andrei, now working for the Soviet secret police, busts an underground speculating ring and nabs Leo, only to discover Kira's clothes in the closet during the arrest. Andrei is deeply shaken, as he realizes that Kira and Leo were pushed into lying and illegal speculation by the practical effects of the very collectivist ideals he admires as a loyal Bolshevik. Under Soviet conditions, their actions were necessary for survival and for love. He arranges for Leo's release and kills himself. A weaselly party functionary reveals Kira's affair with Andrei to Leo, but Leo never learns the reasons for it. He leaves Kira with one of his speculating co-conspirators, out of a general sense of defeat and worthlessness. She makes an effort to flee the country over the Latvian border. She doesn't make it; she is shot and killed in a bored routine way by Ivan Ivanov, a soldier with the Soviet border patrol.

The narrative arc of *We the Living* assigns the bad behavior of Kira, Leo, and their ilk to the conditions created by the Soviets—conditions that prevent them from living fully the higher kind of life they lost, and that they deserve. In contrast, the "mob" of workers (peasants don't generally appear) and the party functionaries are motivated by stupidity, greed, envy, resentment, and bullying brutality. Conditions of life are not explanatory for them. The "collectivist" ideology promoted by the Bolsheviks mobilizes and weaponizes the base motives of the lower orders, and crushes the higher type of potentially creative, achieving individual.

Andrei Taganov is a notable exception. Andrei is the son of a factory owner and a true-believing communist who served with Leon Trotsky in the Red Army during the civil war. He is consistently principled, unlike his comrades. He also bears the marks of the superior individual of Ayn Rand's fictional universe. In her notes on his character in her journal, she writes:

> Dominant trait: a born individualist who never discovered it.... He has an iron will and unconquerable strength.... He has an iron devotion to his ideals, the devotion of a medieval martyr. Capable of anything, any cruelty, if he is convinced that his aim needs it. Cruelty for the cause is, to him, a victory over himself; it gives him the

sense of doing his duty against his sentiments.... The taste, manners, and tact of an aristocrat, but not conventional manners, just the poise and dignity of a man with inborn good judgement.... One of the few people who is absolutely untouched by flattery, admiration, or any form of other people's opinion. Not because of proud disdain, but because of a natural indifference to it. Subconsciously he knows his superiority and does not need anyone's endorsement.[14]

Rand deploys the character of Andrei to address a specific question: Were Bolshevik revolutionary goals admirable, and just the methods objectionable? Or did the goals themselves ultimately require inhumane methods? Andrei Taganov at first serves to show the destructive results of the methods. As does Stepan Timoshenko, another honest Bolshevik character who served with Trotsky, who also kills himself when disillusioned. Though a minor character, Timoshenko is given a highlighted speech denouncing the party's betrayal of the revolution:

You've taken the greatest revolution the world has ever seen and patched the seat of your pants with it.... We started building a temple. Do we end with a chapel? No! And we don't even end with an outhouse. We end with a musty kitchen with a second-hand stove! We set fire under a kettle and we brewed and stirred and mixed blood and fire and steel. What are we fishing now out of the brew? A new humanity? Men of granite? Or at least a good and horrible monster? No! Little puny things that wriggle. Little things that can bend both ways, little double-jointed spirits. Little things that don't even bow humbly to be whipped. No! They take the lash obediently and whip themselves![15]

Ultimately it is Andrei who appears as the tragic figure who finally sees how his idealistic socialist goals lead inexorably to destructive methods. Through Lev, Andrei, and Kira, Rand places the qualities she admires—contempt, aloofness, indifference to others—distinctly within the Russian revolutionary context. Describing Kira in her journal as cruel and sometimes conceited and distant, as well as endowed with "tremendous sexual power,"[16] she shows us Leo in Kira's eyes in the novel: "He was tall; his collar was raised; a cap was pulled over his eyes. His mouth, calm, severe, contemptuous, was that of an ancient chieftain who could order men to die, and his eyes were such as could watch it."[17] These are the qualities of superior individuals that, when constrained by an egalitarian revolutionary ethos, are twisted to antisocial and destructive ends. These are the qualities Rand imagined in the fictional Cyrus Paltons and the living Lev Bekkerman, qualities revealed via powerful physiques fit for imperial and class rule. The other categories of characters in *We the Living* demonstrate varieties of *unfitness:* the scheming ambitious party apparatchiks, the greedy and double-dealing speculators, and the brutal, envious mob. One character who appears at the novel's end provides a key profile of a denizen of the lower orders in this mix—the hapless soldier Ivan Ivanov who shoots Kira in the snow as she crawls toward the border:

> Citizen Ivan Ivanov was six feet tall. He had a wide mouth and a short nose, and when he was puzzled, he blinked, scratching his neck.
>
> Citizen Ivan Ivanov was born in the year 1900, in a basement, in a side street of the town of Vitebsk. He was the ninth child of the family. At the age of six, he started in as apprentice to a shoemaker. The shoemaker beat him with leather suspenders and fed him buckwheat gruel. At the age of ten, he made his first pair of shoes, all by himself, and he wore them proudly down the street, the leather squeaking. That was the first day Citizen Ivan Ivanov remembered all through his life.
>
> At the age of fifteen, he lured the neighborhood's grocer's daughter into a vacant lot and raped her. She was twelve years old, and with a chest as flat as a boy's she whined shrilly. He made her

promise not to tell anyone, and he gave her fifteen kopeks and a pound of sugar candy. That was the second day he remembered.... He served in the Red Army, and, shells roaring overhead, made bets on ice races with the soldiers in the bottom of the trench. He was wounded and told he would die. He stared dully at the wall, for it did not make any difference.

He recovered and married a servant girl with round cheeks and round breasts, because he had gotten her in trouble. Their son was blond and husky, and they named him Ivan. They went to church on Sundays, and his wife cooked onions with roasted mutton, when they could get it. She raised her skirt high over her fat legs and knelt, and scrubbed the white pine floor of their room. And she sent him to a public bath once every month. And Citizen Ivanov was happy....

Citizen Ivanov had never learned to read.[18]

The reader is to understand that this subject of Rand's merciless description, this agent of the Bolshevik revolution, this representative of the mass of humanity, *this* is who killed Kira Argounova. Whether this maliciously cruel depiction of peasant life—degraded, criminally violent, inferior—was shaped in any way by Rand's knowledge of and response to widespread pogroms against Jewish populations in the countryside of the Russian empire, she never says.

Needless to say, the dynamics of empire, the structures of traditional status hierarchies in the countryside and class inequalities in the cities, the history of anti-Semitism, are all absent from the narrative in *We the Living.* Instead we see a topsy-turvy world in which the mass of dull, incapable, and disabled humanity has been mobilized to punish and constrain superior individuals, both those born and nurtured in privilege and those lower born who nonetheless exhibit "aristocratic" qualities.

The gendered nature of this world is manifest via two major strategies: physical and psychological description, and the dynamic of romance. Leading characters are handsome or beautiful, by gender, while the lower types are usually short, fat, or otherwise physically imperfect (according to the imperial ideal) and represented as either malignant or comic. Rand is especially anxious and insistent to distinguish the strong heroic Kira from emerging ideals of revolutionary womanhood. Comrade Sonia, a leader of communist women's groups, is described as unfeminine:

> The young woman had broad shoulders and a masculine leather jacket; short, husky legs and flat, masculine oxfords; a red kerchief tied carelessly over short, straight hair; eyes wide apart in a round, freckled face; thin lips drawn together with so obvious and fierce a discrimination that they seemed weak; dandruff on the black leather of her shoulders.[19]

At the funeral for Andrei near the end of the novel, Comrade Sonia appears again in company:

> … the straight stubby mane of Comrade Sonia waved high in the air, while she roared with all the power of her broad chest about the new duties of the new woman of the Proletariat. Then another face rose over the crowd, a thin, consumptive, unshaved face that wore glasses and opened a pale mouth wide, coughing words which no one could hear.… A tall spinster in a crumpled, old-fashioned hat spoke ferociously, opening her small mouth as if she were at the dentist's, shaking her thin fingers at the crowd as at a school-room of disobedient pupils.[20]

Rand's anxiety to represent an independent female hero, who is nonetheless desirable to the male heroes, may have led her to draw on the European and American movie stars and romance scripts to which she was riveted during her university years. *We the Living* depicts Kira and Leo at the movies, where they note a strong contrast between the Western and Soviet-made films. They see *The Golden Octopus,* an American movie chopped to bits by Soviet censors, though something of its original sparkle peeks through:

> Suddenly, as if a fog had lifted, the photography cleared. They could see the soft line of lipstick and every hair of the long lashes of a beautifully smiling leading lady. Men and women in magnificently foreign clothes moved gracefully.... On the screen, gay people laughed happily, danced in sparkling halls, ran down sandy beaches, their hair in the wind, the muscles of their young arms taut, glistening, monstrously healthy.[21]

Later in the novel, Kira and Andrei go to a foreign film only to find it is sold out, so instead they go into a nearly empty theater to see "The Hit of the Season! New Masterpiece of the Soviet Cinema! Red Warriors, A Gigantic Epic of the Struggle of Red Heroes in the Civil War! A Saga of the Proletariat!," which Kira notes has no hero and no plot. Meanwhile Leo is out at the ballet, seeing "The Dance of the Toilers."[22]

The romance plot of *We the Living* is not unlike the movies, working to balance a riveting female lead's heterosexual and conventional "feminine" appeal with some "modern" independence and sexual freedom. Kira does not intend to marry her lovers, until she becomes desperate and proposes to Leo near the end of the story. But her life force and political commitments are tied completely to her romantic interests, to an extent that is not conceivable for the male characters. As much as Rand admired Pola Negri's full devotion to her art, Kira's devotion to engineering cannot compete with her devotion to Leo. A female hero with that kind of independence would risk crossing over into the masculine or spinster territory of ungendered humor and pathos.

We the Living was not a blockbuster like Rand's later major novels, *The Fountainhead* and *Atlas Shrugged*, though it ultimately sold three million copies worldwide. *We the Living* was also adapted for the stage as *The Unconquered*—a dismal failure produced and directed by George Abbott at the Biltmore Theatre on Broadway in 1940.[23]

In 1942, during the rise of fascism in Europe, the novel was pirated and made into two Italian films directed by Goffredo Alessandrini—*Noi vivi* (We the Living) and *Addio Kira* (Goodbye Kira). Sold as anticommunist propaganda, the films were initially supported by Mussolini's fascist government. *Noi vivi* was shown at the 1942 Venice Film Festival where it not only won the Biennale Prize but also received a standing ovation. The films' reception got complicated after that as audiences and commenters came to detect antifascist themes hiding in plain sight. The German and Italian fascists withdrew their approval, and the director and his assistant fled the country.

Rand's writing sometimes hilariously ridiculed authoritarian pretensions and so appealed to outsiders and iconoclasts. Parts of *We the Living* echo the kind of bitter antiauthoritarian invective found in anarchist Emma Goldman's *My Disillusionment in Russia*, a memoir fully in sympathy with revolutionary collectivism but in sharp opposition to state centralism.[24] The emphasis in the film version shifts somewhat away from the novel's negative portrayals of the mob and toward this critique of an emerging authoritarian state. In the films the antiauthoritarian themes emerged as points of connection with antifascist audiences. The films created a stir all across Europe. Italian audiences began to refer to themselves as Noi Morti (We the Dead), and to the ailing economy as Addio Lira (Goodbye Money). And although her novel was pirated for the film script, Rand eventually approved the English subtitled version.

The strange career of *We the Living* illuminates the differing contexts for reception of Rand's work. During the union mobilizations and emerging social democracies forged in the depression of the 1930s the novel was widely interpreted as an ideological hit piece, hostile to the goals of welfare state liberalism. But by the 1940s in Europe, following the Hitler-Stalin pact of 1939, the film version was widely read as a defense of liberal democracy against both communist and fascist authoritarianism. By 1988, when the English-subtitled film was released during Rand's period of infamy as a marginal reactionary but before her rehabilitation as a neoliberal icon, J. Hoberman opined in the *Village Voice* that the film was "not quite nutty enough to qualify as camp" but was "a unique combination of Adam Smith, Friedrich Nietzsche and Jacqueline Susann." Rand, he noted, "is a triumph of political kitsch."[25]

Certainly *We the Living,* though it remains in print and available on DVD, has not been widely influential in the decades since its publication. But the narrative strategies, characterizations, political morality, and sense of life that Ayn Rand developed during the Russian revolution constituted the vortex of her later whirlwind appeal. *The Fountainhead,* incubated in Hollywood, and *Atlas Shrugged,* hatched in New York City, carried the affective as well as political impact of the Russian revolution forward into new contexts. The characters in *We the Living* are not triumphant heroes, like Howard Roark in *The Fountainhead* and John Galt in *Atlas Shrugged*—they are too closely tied to Rand's bitter, tragic view of the revolution's ruinous impact on the higher type of man and woman. Their cruelty is not yet optimistic. But the astonishing contempt for "others" and indifference to broad social well-being, the outraged sense of entitlement in the face of loss, the hard-edged vision of the "mob" and social inferiors, the celebration of domination, the moralizing contempt for perceived disability and incapacity, the whole structure of feeling that runs throughout Rand's work was forged in counterrevolutionary Russia.

TWO

"Individualists of the World Unite!"

The Fountainhead (1943) was Ayn Rand's first bestseller. The novel marked the author's shift in focus from European "civilization" and the Russian revolution to the industrial United States at midcentury. Tracing the rocky rise of brilliant architect Howard Roark, *The Fountainhead* elaborated central themes of American exceptionalism—up-by-the-bootstraps individualism and dynamic creativity enabled by capitalist freedom. The novel also fully developed Rand's image of the triumphant hero, her outline of the twisted path of feminine aspiration, and her caustic view of the mobs and losers who block the hero and heroine's way. Though set in New York City, the moral economy and structure of feeling featured in *The Fountainhead* derive from Rand's years of living and working in Hollywood. It was there that she first developed a full expression of optimistic cruelty.

Alissa Rosenbaum arrived in New York Harbor in 1926 and soon changed her name to Ayn Rand—a choice that effectively obscured her nationality, gender, and religious origin. Dazzled by the New York skyline, symbolic of the soaring dreams contained in the sheaf of film scenarios she brought with her, she nonetheless soon moved on to Hollywood, where she quickly introduced herself to her favorite director, Cecil B. DeMille. He hired her as an extra on the set of *King of Kings,* where she met another extra, her mesmerizingly handsome future husband, Frank O'Connor. She soon moved into a job as junior script-writer. Within a year of her arrival in Hollywood, she had found her dream job with her dream boss and acquired a suitor seem-ingly sent from central casting to her specifications.[1]

But the young Ayn Rand had no clear idea of where she was, or of the nature of the film business of the 1920s. She arrived in thrall to sparkling images, imagining that life in the United States resembled the life she saw in the movies. She viewed film-making as the creative work of inspired film artists—directors and actors—but did not perceive the evolving corporate form of the emerging industry.

During the 1920s the film industry emerged from the nickelo-deon era, when small theaters catered to working-class and immigrant audiences in U.S. cities, into an era of growth, con-solidation, and expansion to middle-class audiences. By the end of World War I the Hollywood film moguls were global leaders running corporations that combined production, distribution, and exhibition in order to maintain control of an orderly market. By 1930, eight Hollywood studios controlled 95 percent of the industry revenues, generally administered from corporate offices in New York. According to film historians Douglas Gomery and Lee Grieveson, the studio system emerged in the 1930s as a col-lusive oligopoly, financed by major investment banks and with near-monopoly control of global film distribution.[2]

The moguls came to Los Angeles because of the weather, the abundance of possible film locations, and because labor was largely unorganized and cheap. During the 1920s they faced the challenges of labor unrest and domestic and foreign government restrictions on content and distribution. They organized to meet those challenges through the Motion Picture Producers and Distributors of America (MPPDA, also known as the Hays Office), established in 1922, and the Academy of Motion Picture Arts and Sciences, established in 1927. The Academy served as a "company union" for writers, actors, and directors. The studios had labor agreements with many of the nine-to-five workers in the industry—carpenters, stage hands, musicians, and others— but broader unionization did not challenge the studio system until the 1930s.

On this hardnosed business foundation, the movies emerged as a major twentieth-century national-imperial culture industry, "Americanizing" the world from Hollywood and New York. On a foundation of labor struggles, monopoly power, and government deal-making the film industry created the glittering surface of the movies. Increasingly marketing to middle-class audiences, the studios began to produce feature films built on the star system. They participated centrally in creating the modes of production, distribution, and mass consumption characteristic of emerging U.S.-based global corporate capitalism. Corporate forms constructed with finance capital replaced small-scale industry; U.S. economic imperialism supplemented, then supplanted, the predominantly territorial strategies of the British empire.

This American culture industry was built by immigrants—at the top, primarily by eastern European Jewish moguls. Stridently assimilationist, these businessmen generally downplayed their past in an embrace of their new country. According to film scholars, these creative outsiders manufactured an American

Dream fantasy machine—a machine that idealized the United States by erasing its settler colonial origins, imperial aspirations, and stark capitalist inequalities. Having been excluded from other major industries by anti-immigrant and anti-Semitic restrictions, these ambitious entrepreneurs moved into the film business when there was a low bar to entry. They developed it into a major economic powerhouse by selling fantasies of glittering prosperity and glamour, of heroic white American conquest and industry.

The movies emerged as the dominant mass-cultural form at a crucial moment in nation formation: after the Civil War, Reconstruction, and the closing of the American "frontier"; during the first stirrings of U.S. imperial expansion abroad; and at the height of mass immigration. The movies outlined the cultural terms of national consolidation at the turn of the century. D.W. Griffith's *The Birth of a Nation* (1915) became a key text in the birth of twentieth-century racial capitalism by broadcasting the logic of American apartheid known as "Jim Crow." Its representations of black former slaves as threatening to the peace of the republic promoted a newly unified, aggressive, but noble national whiteness. Alongside other genre movies, it set the boundaries of this American whiteness through exclusion—westerns featured Americans vs. Native Americans and Mexicans, historical epics exoticized Asians and the Middle Easterners, blackface comedies extended the exclusion of African Americans.

American whiteness allowed the assimilation of European "ethnic" immigrants, including eventually, if ambivalently, eastern European Jews—though class and gender distinctions continued to matter. White women of the respectable classes were represented as sources of morality, or increasingly as lures for consumption—but with more contradictory complexity than nonwhite people of either gender. Meanwhile the decision makers behind the camera and in the business office were overwhelmingly men of European descent.[3]

Ayn Rand arrived on the scene in Hollywood without any clear understanding of the mode of business or the politics of representation developing there. Her initial astounding successes, dependent in part on her ability to assimilate as white, felt to her like pure individual achievement. Then she quickly ran into trouble that she could not comprehend. She arrived as Cecil B. DeMille's adoring fan, but later dismissed him as a "box office chaser"—a dismissal signaling her failure to grasp the nature of the movies as an industry, where the motor powering profits was precisely box office chasing.

Rand's belief in the crucial role of pure talent and energized aspiration was severely challenged during 1927 and '28, when the rise of the talkies rendered her imperfect English a distinct disadvantage. No longer able to find work in the film industry, she turned to odd jobs to pay her rent. It was during this period of dark despair that she wrote the character profile based on murderer William Hickman. She began to express disillusionment with Americans, finding mediocrity, conformity, and envy surrounding her. The reality of Hollywood as a land of hardscrabble business dealings that now affected her negatively dented her glittering fantasies of pure individual creative achievement. She reacted not by reorganizing her perceptions in accordance with her experience, but rather by attacking the people around her as disappointments and failures. It wasn't the dynamics of capitalism that were to blame for "box office chasing"; instead, mediocre and morally compromised people betrayed the ideal of capitalism as the best engine of creativity.[4]

The decade of the 1920s ended with the economic crash that inaugurated the Great Depression, but an upward swing began for Rand. In 1929, afraid that her visa would soon expire, she married part-time actor Frank O'Connor and gained permanent residency; she became a U.S. citizen a few years later. She landed a secure job in the RKO women's wardrobe department. Then in the 1930s she wrote and sold her film script *Red Pawn*, staged her play *The Night of January 16th* in Hollywood and New York, published *We the Living* and her dystopian novella *Anthem*, wrote the novelette and stage versions of *Ideal* (published only posthumously), and began work on her first major success, the novel *The Fountainhead.*

Alongside this productivity Rand began to focus her attention on U.S. politics. Although she had voted for Franklin Delano Roosevelt for president in 1932, largely because he promised to end Prohibition, she soon regretted that vote. As the influence of John Maynard Keynes increased and the outlines of the New Deal welfare state emerged, Rand felt increasingly embattled. She discerned the spread of "collectivism" and sympathy for the Soviets in the United States, especially in the movie and publishing worlds. She believed she was being shut out all through the so-called Red Decade and Popular Front years, for her attacks on communism and defense of capitalism.[5]

Rand moved to New York City in 1934 to work with the Broadway producer of *Night of January 16th*. From then until 1943, when she moved back to California to work on the film production of *The Fountainhead,* she made connections with the extensive network of "FDR haters." Her new engagements distracted her from the always difficult writing of her novel. Rand plunged headlong into the Wendell Wilkie campaign for president in an effort to deny FDR a third term. Although the Wilkie campaign failed, Rand greatly expanded her network of anti–New Dealers in New York. She enjoyed speaking to the public in various venues, declaring, "I was a marvelous propagandist!" After Wilkie lost, Rand proposed an anti–New Deal organization and drafted a statement of principles, "The Individualist Manifesto" (her first extended piece of nonfiction writing), intended to provide procapitalist forces with a galvanizing statement equivalent to *The Communist Manifesto.*[6]

This political whirlwind was interrupted when she signed a contract with Bobbs-Merrill for her novel, with a firm due date of January 1, 1943. She withdrew to work furiously, powered in part by the amphetamine Benzedrine, upon which she depended for three decades. She met the deadline. *The Fountainhead* was published in 1943 along with two other books by women, both friends of Rand's, considered foundational for modern right-wing capitalist libertarianism: Isabel Paterson's *The God of the Machine* and Rose Wilder Lane's *The Discovery of Freedom.*[7] Sales were slow over the summer but picked up in the fall despite generally unfavorable reviews. Word of mouth eventually propelled *The Fountainhead* into a publishing legend, with sales increasing exponentially and sustained at an exceptionally high level to the present day. Ayn Rand became famous, attracting mountains of fan mail and intensifying public attention. By the end of 1943 she had sold the film rights and moved back to Hollywood with Frank.

At the house they bought in Chatsworth, a glass and steel modernist structure designed by Richard Neutra for Josef Sternberg and Marlene Dietrich, Rand's attentions often wandered from her "hero" Frank to an array of young men who visited her there to discuss philosophy and *The Fountainhead*. But as World War II ended, Rand was again drawn into politics. This time, rather than being among a minority of "free marketeers" stridently opposed to the New Deal, she joined an emerging formation of virulently anticommunist Cold Warriors.

The year 1947 was a crucial one in the shift from a New Deal to a Cold War context in the United States. Ayn Rand was a founding member and served on the executive committees of two Hollywood-based anticommunist organizations, the Motion Picture Alliance for the Preservation of American Ideals (MPA) and the American Writers' Association. MPA was supported by a heavyweight crew including John Wayne, Walt Disney, Gary Cooper, Ronald Reagan, Cecil B. DeMille, Ginger Rogers, Hedda Hopper, and Barbara Stanwyck. The organization drew up a list of friendly witnesses for the House Un-American Activities Committee (HUAC), including Rand. She also published a "Screen Guide for Americans" in the magazine *Plain Talk* that was summarized in the Sunday *New York Times*.[8] In it she advised movie producers and executives to eschew left-wing influence by refusing to smear success or glorify the common man.

In her public testimony before HUAC in October 1947, Rand again demonstrated that she did not really understand where she was, or the dynamics of the industry-government dance pervading the context of the hearings. From the start of the anticommunist investigations, the Hollywood moguls negotiated the complex interplay of anticommunism and anti-Semitism. Capitalists to the core, they nonetheless understood the strain of anti-Semitism in the anti-pink fervor—the assumption that communists were Jewish, and Jews were communists. They feared that cooperating with the inquests would energize attacks that would ultimately bring them down. So they resisted, to a limited degree. The Jewish moguls did not join Rand's MPA, which was peppered with known anti-Semites. The pressure on them ultimately produced a defensive strategy of identifying a few communist-influenced writers and directors (and ultimately blacklisting them), while insisting that their films, and their industry in general, were free of significant communist influence. They deflected criticism of the industry's business practices via their willingness to scapegoat and destroy the careers and livelihoods of employees and colleagues, many of them also Jewish. They also collaborated with government as they always had, in promoting and regulating movies for the domestic and global markets. In this case they rather cannily used HUAC to gain more control over their employees and unions.[9]

Ayn Rand never fully grasped this situation. She ultimately alienated moguls and HUAC committee members with scathing, unnuanced testimony attacking popular films and the industry as infiltrated by communism. She was not asked back for the second day of testimony, and she was widely vilified in the press—for denouncing a film as politically suspect because it showed Russians smiling.

Meanwhile Joan Crawford, Barbara Stanwyck, and Veronica Lake lobbied Rand for the role of Dominique Francon in *The Fountainhead*, and Clark Cable and Humphrey Bogart pushed to play Howard Roark—before the lead roles were given to Patricia Neal and Gary Cooper. The film opened to moderate box office and poor reviews in 1949. Though pleased with the film at the close of its production, Rand became bitterly disappointed with it after its release. Nonetheless, *The Fountainhead* ultimately made her reputation and changed her life.

During the 1930s and '40s, Rand produced novels, plays, and screenplays. She wrote the novelette *Ideal* in 1934 and reworked it into a play in 1936, and she penned another play in 1939, *Think Twice*. (These were not published or produced during her lifetime.) A few of her screenplays—all adaptations except for *Red Pawn*—became movies, including *Love Letters,* with Jennifer Jones and John Cotton, and *You Came Along,* with Robert Cummings and Lizabeth Scott (both produced by Hal Wallis for Paramount in 1945). But her major work, the one that launched her into popular fame and iconic status on the right, was her nearly seven-hundred-page novel *The Fountainhead.*

During two breaks in the research and writing for that novel Rand wrote *Anthem* (1938), a dystopian futuristic novella, and "The Individualist Manifesto" (typescript 1941), later revised and published in the *Reader's Digest* as "The Only Path to Tomorrow" (1946). These publications reached backward and forward, marking a significant transition in Rand's thinking that shaped *The Fountainhead* as she wrote.

Anthem portrays a future society in which equality is enforced by a World Council, and the concept of the individual, the word *I* itself, has been abolished. The text is the diary of Equality 7–2521, whose love of the Science of Things is discouraged by the Council of Vocations. To stamp out any sense of superiority, Equality (always referred to with plural pronouns) is assigned to life as a Street Sweeper. Like any worthy Rand hero, "they" are male, young, tall, and handsome in a muscular, square-jawed Aryan way, and drawn to a gorgeous blonde female, Liberty 5–3000.

The World Council presides over a society that has regressed into another primitive Dark Age without the technology and progress characteristic of the Unmentionable Time before. Those who stray from the will of the Council are severely punished by lash or burning at the stake in the Palace of Corrective Detention. When Equality (re)discovers electricity, they are declared evil and sent to be whipped. Needless to say, Rand's bitter parody of the physically unattractive Council members sends them up as purely evil embodiments of "collectivist" bureaucracy. Their pronouncements on Equality's light box are hilarious to any reader, from any political perspective, annoyed by bureaucrats:

> What is not done collectively cannot be good....
> This box will bring ruin to the Department of Candles. It took fifty years to secure the approval of all the councils for the candle....
> If this light should lessen the toil of men, then it is a great evil....
> For men have no cause to exist save for toiling for other men.[10]

Anthem, like *We the Living* and *Red Pawn,* draws on Rand's experience in Russia, and may have been influenced by a Russian futuristic novel by Yevgeny Zamyatin, *We,* that circulated in Russia during 1921 (published in English translation in 1924). But Rand's novella did differ from Zamyatin's (and from Aldous Huxley's 1932 novel *Brave New World*) in one key respect: Zamyatin cast his dystopia as technologically sophisticated.[11] Rand's future society has regressed into a second Dark Age, due to the eradication of individual initiative by the World Council. This portrayal fit with Rand's imperial view and civilizational discourse. For her, only individualist capitalism can support innovation and progress. She usually avoided explicitly racializing this discourse, perhaps because she was fully aware of the rise of fascism in Europe and of the anti-Semitism that fascist racial policy was explicitly promoting there. But her endorsement of civilizational discourse, and her belief in historical progress from primitive barbarism to civilization through European empire, conveyed implicit racial assumptions. Her physical descriptions attached Aryan good looks to intelligence and creativity. All of her characters were of European descent, though their worthiness varied according to physical differences. The civilizational framework and the character descriptions in *Anthem* are inscribed in a pervasive hierarchy of mental and physical ability that intertwines with racial, class, and moral differences in all Rand's fiction.

This belief in the inherent moral as well as technological inferiority of "primitive" societies shaped her response to the concern of a Native American cadet at West Point in 1974. The cadet asked her how she squared her beliefs with the historical record of dispossession and extermination of American Indians. She replied that the Indians had had the land for five thousand years and had done nothing with it, saying further that "it is always going to transpire that when a superior technological culture meets up with an inferior one, the superior will prevail."[12]

Anthem is somewhat of an anomaly in Rand's body of work in its representation of gender and reproduction. Liberty is described as an ideal Randian imperial subject, whose eyes showed "no fear in them, no kindness and no guilt." But she is also monogamous and reproductive—pregnant by Equality at the end of the novella. This sentimental romance-to-maternity plotline stands alone in Rand's original fiction, to be replaced later by intensely eroticized romantic triangles, no pregnancies in sight.[13]

Anthem was the last of Rand's writings to clearly reference the Russian context. The novella creates a cartoon version of the Russian revolutionary present, portrayed as taking humanity back to the "dark ages" of the Russian empire's feudal past. The text also points forward toward "civilization," the modernizing capitalist West. And it was from this new location that she launched her future polemics.

Rand penned the first extended nonfiction explication of her evolving political philosophy in 1941. "The Individualist Manifesto" mirrors *The Communist Manifesto,* complete with the call

"Individualists of the World Unite!" The manifesto reflects Rand's experience in the Wilkie campaign and the impact of her recent engagement with Isabel Paterson, a novelist, conservative anti–New Deal political philosopher, and author of a widely read book review column in the *New York Herald Tribune.* Paterson included Rand in her Monday night discussion salons and became the younger woman's only real mentor. Through Paterson, Rand encountered the British and American individualist tradition and began to shed her Nietzschean elitist contempt for a more Americanized version based more on merit than on nature (though nature persisted in Rand's aristocratic, imperial physical descriptions). There is no evidence that she read widely or deeply in the original political philosophical texts, but at Paterson's salon she encountered secondary and derivative literature.[14]

The manifesto echoes the U.S. Declaration of Independence, as well as ideas and language derived from widely influential writers including social Darwinist Herbert Spencer. Although she argues that the nineteenth-century defense of capitalism desperately needs updating, the manifesto repeats earlier ideas, slogans, and concepts. The thirty-two-page document endorses "Life, Liberty and the Pursuit of Happiness," achievable only through capitalism. Echoing *Anthem,* she portrays "collectivism" as a return to the "dark ages," dominated by Passive Man. Active Man, whose principal aspect is Individual Freedom, is to lead humanity forward.[15]

The Fountainhead was Ayn Rand's big breakout book, through which she built a fan base, political influence, and popular readership. It constituted her first ambitious attempt to provide a defense of individualism and capitalism in a mid-twentieth-century context. Read in relation to Rand's experience in Hollywood, the novel presents an analysis of U.S. corporate capitalism that is at once profoundly deformed and distorted, yet deeply effective at providing an energizing rationale for American business interests. *The Fountainhead* offered simultaneously eroticized and moralized character studies embedded in a heroic romance plot, for the purpose of generating desire for capitalism.

Howard Roark is the heroic modernist architect at the center of *The Fountainhead.* Based on Frank Lloyd Wright, Roark was Rand's first full-fledged triumphant hero. Her physical descriptions of him echo her earlier "superior" male characters: "His face was like a law of nature—a thing one could not question, alter or implore. It had high cheekbones over gaunt, hollow cheeks; gray eyes, cold and steady; a contemptuous mouth, shut tight, the mouth of an executioner, or a saint."[16] This manly hero, a kind of conquistador figure dominant over nature and other people, has no friends and family and, rather like Rand's descriptions of serial killer William Hickman in her journal, "had never learned the process of thinking about other people." In her journal she adds, "Indifference and an infinite, calm contempt is all he feels for the world and for other men who are not like him."[17]

Roark's rugged appeal is contrasted with more conventional male attractiveness, a soft handsomeness possessed by the character Peter Keating, the popular man who seeks to please—a "second hander" in Rand's damning view. We know he is weak because he loves his overbearing mother for no reason other than that she is his mother. In her journal Rand describes him as distinctly feminine: "Graceful, with the studied perfect, too soft and fluent grace of a ballet dancer.... Very pretty hands, always perfectly groomed.... Long thin nose and a very small mouth, delicate, flower-like and pretty, inclined to pout in a 'bee-stung' manner, a mouth that would be small and pretty even on a girl."[18]

Other characters created to contrast with Roark include Gail Wynand, editor of the tabloid the *Banner,* modeled on William Randolph Hearst—an ambitious businessman who sells his soul to pander to the "mob" that reads his newspaper. The villain Ellsworth Toohey, architecture critic at the *Banner,* is a union promoter and effete intellectual based partly on Rand's observations of British socialist Harold Laski. Rand's description in her journal bears the marks of common anti-Semitic representations:

> Toohey's physical appearance: medium height, rather on the short-ish side, skinny, anemic, concave-chested, spindly, slightly bow-legged, ridiculous and offensive in a bathing suit. A glaring lack of vitality—compensated, so he thinks, by his intellectual achievements. Long narrow face, slightly receding chin, protruding upper teeth, in a sharp circular rodent fashion—not too good a set of teeth, nor too clean.[19]

These characters are set into motion in a plot designed to reveal their essential natures. The nearly seven hundred pages of *The Fountainhead* offer numerous plot twists but no real surprises as everyone behaves according to highly stylized type—up to the dramatic ending when the hero, Roark, blows up a public housing project because the developers and other architects have compromised and corrupted his architectural vision. He goes on trial, delivers a marathon polemic, and is acquitted.

The female romantic lead character, Dominique Francon, comes across as secondary to this didactic plot. Her physical description places her clearly within Rand's Aryan feminine ideal: "Her slender body seemed out of all scale in relation to a normal human body; its lines were so long, so fragile, so exaggerated that she looked like a stylized drawing of a woman and made the correct proportions of a normal being appear heavy and awkward beside her."[20] Dominique is *The Fountainhead*'s only conflicted, inconsistent, and unpredictable character. Once described by Rand as "myself on a bad day," she is a fiercely independent newspaper columnist at her father's newspaper, the *Banner*. She knows Roark is her true love and hero but rejects him and tortures him by marrying Keating, then Wynand, all the while attacking her hero's work. This love-hate relationship is motivated by Dominique's belief that Roark will be broken by the world. She would rather reject him, or induce him to withdraw from architecture, than see him ruined. It is through this conflict that Rand works to resolve the contradiction between a heroic independent woman and the proper femininity of the heterosexually active heroine, desiring and desirable in a male-dominated romantic context. Rand relies on sadomasochistic desire to endow Dominique with an active ferocious ambivalent desire fulfilled only by submission to the ideal man, Roark.

The most cited scene in *The Fountainhead* is the conquest of Dominique by Roark, often referred to as the "rape scene." Susan Brownmiller, author of *Against Rape* (1975), reports preparing to read the novel in the New York Public Library and finding that the volume fell open to that scene, apparently lingered over by legions of readers before her.[21] Rand later described this scene as "rape by engraved invitation," or as consensual, pointedly desired, domination and submission: "He did it as an act of scorn. Not as love, but as defilement. And this made her still and submit. One gesture of tenderness from him—and she would have remained cold, unreached by the thing done to her body. But the act of a master taking shameful, contemptuous possession of her was the kind of rapture she wanted."[22] Rand explains in her journal:

> Dominique's basic passion is a fierce love of independence. But it is an independence that turns in upon itself—in protest against the world she sees around her. Capable of great desire, she makes it her

aim to desire nothing. Actually a saint, in that her subconscious demand is perfection—from herself and from all others—she finds a vicious delight in lowering herself to whatever action she considers most contemptible; since she cannot find perfection, she prefers its opposite extreme to compromise....

... Like most women, and to a greater degree than most, she is a masochist and she wishes for the happiness of suffering at Roark's hands. Sexually, Roark has a great deal of the sadist, and he finds pleasure in breaking her will and her defiance. Yet he loves her, and this love is the only passion for another human being in his whole life. And her love for him is essentially worship, it becomes her religion, it becomes her reconciliation with life, with humanity and with herself—but not until many years later.[23]

Dominique's marriages to Keating and Wynand produce romantic triangles like those in *We the Living* and *Red Pawn*. The Wynand-Dominique-Roark connections in particular support Eve Sedgwick's argument in *Between Men* that such triangles deploy the heterosexual relation to desexualize the homoerotic bond between the men. The existence of the heterosexual relation provides the homoerotic connection with sexual deniability.[24] Rand noted in her journal:

Wynand is actually in love with Roark. It is love in every sense but the physical; its base is not in homosexuality. Wynand has never had any tendency in that direction. It is more hero-worship than love, and more religion that hero-worship. Actually, it is Wynand's tribute to his own unrealized greatness.... Wynand welcomes the torture of loving a man whom he should hate.[25]

Rand's treatments of gender are not the only ambivalent representations in the text. Though her physical descriptions carry coded anti-Semitism throughout, the strong outsider identification of her hero, and his persecution by a fresh-faced American boy among others, may reflect a sense of outsiderness acquired and intensified into anger and hatred in violently anti-Semitic Russia. Her central theme of outsiders struggling against unjust persecution by complacent, entitled mediocrities might also illuminate some part of the wide appeal of her fiction. Though her representations of "the mob" began to shift somewhat during the writing of *The Fountainhead,* the persecuting mob of her contemptuous imagination can be found whipped up by the tabloid headlines in the *Banner.* But the jury that acquits Roark at the end also represents "the common man." Like the crowds that cheered Rand on during the Wilkie campaign, this jury can recognize greatness in Roark, and can be fair. Her salon intensives on American individualism with Isabel Paterson, attended while on hiatus from the novel, may have tempered her hatred of the inferior hordes. They certainly motivated her to reject Nietzsche and remove his quotes from the start of her chapters.[26]

The Fountainhead sold slowly at first and received mixed reviews. Two reviews in the *New York Times* demonstrate the range of responses. On May 12, 1943, the paper's regular book reviewer, Orville Prescott, noted that "Miss Rand must have a hidden dynamo of superhuman energy purring inside her head. Her book is so highly charged it seems to vibrate and emit a shower of sparks." (He probably didn't know about her Benzedrine habit.) He continued,

> All the betrayals, all the dirty crawling, scheming malice, all the lust and lechery in "The Fountainhead" give it an atmosphere so luridly evil and conspiratorial that Cesare Borgia, the Marquis de Sade and Adolf Hitler could walk right in and feel cozily at home. The result is disastrous to what I am sure are Miss Rand's high and solemn intentions. The coils and convolutions of her plot are complicated and violent enough to have an interest of their own, but the interest is rather like that aroused by a Boris Karloff movie. Miss Rand's crude cast of characters are just about exactly on that level.[27]

No doubt Rand believed that such a reviewer did not understand her "romantic realism," her reliance on ideal types and clashes of values that she learned from her devotion to Victor Hugo, and her rejection of the kind of naturalistic writing held in high regard among critics. But on May 16, the Sunday *New York Times* ran an adulatory review by feminist psychologist and former Smith College professor Lorine Pruette: "Ayn Rand is a writer of great power. She has a subtle and ingenious mind and the capacity of writing brilliantly, beautifully, bitterly.... Good novels of ideas are rare at any time. This is the only novel of ideas written by an American woman that I can recall."[28]

Sales of *The Fountainhead* picked up after summer 1943, and by the end of the year it had sold more than 100,000 copies, a rate of sale that only rose year by year, generated mostly by word of mouth. The total sales as of this writing exceed six and a half million copies. The book was a publishing phenomenon—a fat novel full of long, didactic speeches that became a bestseller! Fan letters began pouring in to Rand's publisher, eventually by the thousands. As Rand biographer Jennifer Burns reports, readers recounted their experiences of *revelation* and *awakening* upon reading the novel. It was indeed Rand's intention to stir her readers' deep emotions in keeping with her belief that procapitalist forces needed to copy the left by appealing to them on a deeper level than mere politics. Although readers' reactions did not always follow the lines Rand preferred, deep reactions of some kind were widely reported.[29]

The Fountainhead joined a short list of popular American novels with political resonance and huge sales that rose above the category of "genre novel" but were nonetheless held in generally low regard by literary critics. Like *Uncle Tom's Cabin* and *Gone with the Wind*, *The Fountainhead* ultimately became what scholar Linda

Williams has called a "trans genre media event," with its multiple editions, a magazine serialization, and a Hollywood movie.[30]

During the mid-1940s, the political atmosphere was shifting as the world war ended and the Cold War ramped up. Rand's ideas moved from the margins toward the center of U.S. political life. Her novel fit into the new zeitgeist and continued doing very well, even if the movie version did not. But *The Fountainhead* took shape in earlier decades, during her life in Hollywood in the 1920s and '30s. Seen as a kind of crude mirror of Rand's view of Hollywood, translated from filmmaking to architecture, *The Fountainhead* presents the independent professional (Roark, Rand) at loggerheads with mediocre colleagues ("architecture by committee," producers and directors), at the mercy of a large media corporation (the *Banner,* the studios), and under attack by collectivists (Toohey, the Reds of Hollywood). Gail Wynand's tragic fate echoes Rand's view of Cecil B. DeMille, the great director ruined by box office chasing.

Rand does provide a critique of capitalism in *The Fountainhead,* but it is a critique from the right. It is a critique of actually-existing capitalism as impure, as infested with Reds and on the collectivizing path to hell. She is a central figure in the development and spread of a political formation that historian Lee Grieveson calls "militant liberalism." Grieveson traces this formation from 1919, in the wake of the Bolshevik revolution and World War I, through an intensification from the margins in opposition to progressive social democracy in the 1930s, to the Cold War. He then identifies militant liberalism as the core of neoliberal thinking in the 1970s and '80s.[31]

In *The Reactionary Mind,* Corey Robin argues that the diverse and clashing threads of right-wing opinion cohere on two points:

the defense of hierarchy and the attack on, and appropriation of, the strategies of the left.[32] Rand's writing fits this framework well. Her ideas and feelings emerged during the Bolshevik revolution, when her sense of outraged entitlement in the face of (to her) undeserved loss congealed into a moral economy and a structure of feeling that shaped her life's work. Her impassioned defense of hierarchy, embedded in the history of racial capitalism and imperialism, combined with a eugenic sense of the greater value of physical beauty and capacity, infused her sense of superiority with moral righteousness. The resulting commitments shaped her lifelong advocacy of militant liberalism, or unregulated capitalism. To advance this advocacy, Rand repeatedly borrows ideas and language from the left. "Individuals of the World Unite!" may be contradictory, but it is typical of her constant appropriation of socialist strategies.

Rand wanted to borrow and counter socialist feelings as well as ideas. The aspirations and achievements of Ayn Rand's heroes and heroines, combined with contempt and indifference for social inferiors, formed the structure of feeling she endlessly circulated for decades to come—*optimistic cruelty,* a practice as well as a feeling, set against the feeling of *solidarity* that runs through and nurtures the egalitarian social movements she so ferociously opposed.

THREE

"Would You Cut the Bible?"

Atlas Shrugged is Ayn Rand's magnum opus. Published in 1957 after thirteen years of sometimes tortured, often amphetamine-fueled effort, the massive thousand-plus-page novel provoked polarized responses that illuminated the conflicts shaping the postwar political world. Reviled by mainstream critics, adored by a reverential following and an expanding mass-reading public, the book became a touchstone that continues to shape political and popular culture into the present day. But during the years of its creation, Rand herself was an increasingly isolated figure on the fringes of intellectual life in the United States.

In 1930s and '40s California and New York, Rand fell in with the relatively small minority of right-wing defenders of unregulated capitalism. She actively opposed the New Deal, especially via the Wilkie campaign. She joined in antiunion activity in Hollywood and fanned the anticommunist fervor surrounding her testimony before HUAC. She expounded right-wing attacks on the emerging postwar political consensus in favor of a so-called mixed economy—capitalist enterprises constrained by government regulation, organized labor, and an expanding safety net of public support for the needy. Ayn Rand's motley band of "free market" capitalist agitators had some successes. They supported the 1947 Taft-Hartley Act that limited the rights of labor unions and eroded protections that organized labor had won under the 1935 Wagner Act. They promoted investigations and blacklists. But proponents of laissez-faire capitalism felt profoundly embattled during the 1950s and '60s. Support for government-regulated business, organized labor, and welfare state programs like Social Security was deeply entrenched by the time of the 1952 victory of "moderate" Dwight Eisenhower over right-wing senator Robert Taft (cosponsor of the Taft-Hartley Act) for the Republican presidential nomination. Yet although regulated capitalism was decidedly still capitalism, and the welfare state was not a socialist one, Rand and her zealous colleagues refused to make that distinction. (For a broader discussion of the welfare state and its critics, see chapter 4.)

The "radicals for capitalism" remained a distinct minority during the 1950s, and they were a fractious bunch. Business owners had begun organizing against state regulation and unionization in the 1930s, establishing institutions like Leonard Read's Foundation for Economic Education and Harold Luhnow's reorganized Volker Fund in the 1940s. Such institutions provided support and spread the ideas of Austrian School free-market economists Ludwig von Mises and Friedrich Hayek. The nascent libertarian movement ultimately claimed these economists as founders, along with three popular novelists who published key nonfiction texts in 1943: Isabel Patterson, *God in the Machine;* Rose Wilder Lane, *The Discovery of Freedom;* and Ayn Rand, *The Fountainhead.* But the ranks were replete with evolving political tiffs and personal feuds—between anti-state free marketeers and cold warriors allied with the state, between atheists and religious traditionalists, between advocates of a minimal state and anarchists.[1]

When William F. Buckley founded the *National Review* in 1955, he hoped to chart a path to power for his favored respectable religious conservatives, over and against New Dealers and Republican "moderates" like Eisenhower but also versus fellow travelers on the political right—fanatical anticommunists and purist laissez-faire advocates. Looking back in his 2003 partially fact-based "novel" *Getting It Right,* he painted a smug, triumphalist picture of mainstream conservative victories, including over the right-wing fringe John Birch Society and Rand's crew of free-market true believers. But this outcome could not have seemed inevitable during the 1950s.[2]

At least as fractious as her fellow procapitalist activists, Ayn Rand progressively withdrew from the fray of intellectual social life among colleagues during the 1950s. As she labored long hours on her novel, she became increasingly dependent on a social, cultural, and intellectual world constructed for her by her primary acolyte, Nathan Blumenthal. A child of Russian Jewish Canadians, Blumenthal was twenty-five years younger than Rand. He began reading and rereading *The Fountainhead* from the age of fourteen, memorizing whole sections. After enrolling at UCLA along with his girlfriend Barbara Weidman, he received a response to his fan letters and an invitation to visit Rand at her California manse. They all moved to New York in 1951—Ayn and Frank, Nathan and Barbara—and co-created the small circle that became the base camp for Rand's philosophical movement, Objectivism.

The weird little group of Rand followers became known, with deliberate irony, as the Collective, or as the Class of '43 (publication year of *The Fountainhead*). Devoted to a philosophy that emphasized atheism and devalued purely biological or "ethnic" ties in favor of more "rational" associations, the Collective was composed almost entirely of the Russian Jewish relatives and childhood friends (and their partners and spouses) of Blumenthal and Weidman. Like the Hollywood moguls Rand left behind in California, these Rand acolytes were at odds in many ways with their families of origin, but nonetheless shared affinities of background and experience that drew them into a chosen association. Also like the Hollywood gang, their experiences of "foreignness" and exclusion sharpened their idealizations of American history and commerce. Yet these advocates of fierce individual independence met weekly to read and praise Rand's novel, chapter by chapter. Their leader, who created heroic figures of masculine achievement and described herself as a "man worshiper," financially supported a charming, passive, exquisitely dressed husband who rarely spoke at Collective meetings and worked intermittently as a florist and then later as a painter. The ferocious believer in integrity, honesty, and undeniable, objective reality who guided and judged the Collective's members kept a corrosive secret that ultimately destroyed the group: she began an affair with Nathan Blumenthal, who changed his name to Nathaniel Branden and married Barbara Weidman in 1953.[3]

When *Atlas Shrugged* made its incendiary appearance in 1957, it cracked open the apparent political consensus in favor of the welfare state to reveal intensely warring camps. The mainstream press, leading academics, and prominent literary figures didn't just dismiss the tome; they *abhorred* it. Rand herself predicted to Nathaniel Branden that her novel was "going to be the most controversial book of this century; I'm going to be hated, vilified, lied about, smeared in every possible way."[4] Her characteristic grandiosity notwithstanding, she was prescient. *Atlas Shrugged* was described as "execrable claptrap," "grotesque eccentricity," and a "shrill diatribe" comparable in its godless, heartless over-wrought cruelty to Nietzschean-inflected fascism.[5] Ex-Communist but still left-leaning literary critic Granville Hicks opined in the *New York Times*, "It howls in the reader's ear and beats him about the head in order to secure his attention. And then, when it has him subdued, harangues him for page upon page. It has only two moods, the melodramatic and the didactic, and in both it knows no bounds."[6]

But the most notoriously devastating review came from William Buckley's *National Review*. Echoing the views of many religious conservatives, another kind of ex-Communist slammed Rand for her atheism and lack of charity and compassion. In "Big Sister Is Watching You," Whittaker Chambers wrote that *Atlas Shrugged* substitutes "the Sign of the Dollar, in lieu of the Sign of the Cross," presenting the "Randian Man" who, like "Marxian Man," is at "the center of a godless world." Chambers continues: "Out of a lifetime of reading, I can recall no other book in which a tone of overriding arrogance was so implacably sustained. Its shrillness is without reprieve. Its dogmatism is without appeal.... From almost any page of *Atlas Shrugged*, a voice can be heard from painful necessity, commanding: 'To a gas chamber—go!'"[7]

These over-the-top negative reviews combined bitter rejection of Ayn Rand's philosophy, from the right as well as the left, with attacks on the crudeness of the writing style and on the tone or sheer meanness of the novel. They were met with a much smaller number of equally over-the-top positive reviews and private evaluations, deeming *Atlas Shrugged* "vibrant and powerful" and Rand a writer of "dazzling virtuosity." Economist Ruth Alexander, Rand's friend, predicted that "Ayn Rand is destined to rank in history as the outstanding novelist and most profound philosopher of the twentieth century."[8] A private note to the author from famed right-wing economist Ludwig von Mises praised the book as a political achievement:

> *Atlas Shrugged* is not merely a novel.... It is also—or may I say: first of all—a cogent analysis of the evils that plague our society, a substantiated rejection of the ideology of our self-styled "intellectuals" and a pitiless unmasking of the insincerity of the policies adopted by our governments and political parties. It is a devastating exposure of the "moral cannibals," the "gigolos of science," and of the "academic prattle" of the makers of the "anti-industrial revolution."[9]

Time magazine summarized the overall reception of the novel by asking, "Is it a novel? Is it a nightmare?"[10]

Despite the overwhelmingly negative reviews in the mainstream press, *Atlas Shrugged* quickly became a word-of-mouth bestseller, generating thousands of fan letters from gushing enthusiasts.[11] Though never regarded as serious by cultural gatekeepers, the novel nonetheless became undeniably socially and politically important, sometimes compared to *Uncle Tom's Cabin, Gone with the Wind,* and *1984.* How could a thousand-plus-page novel, featuring cartoonish characters moving through a melodramatic plot peppered with long didactic speeches, attract so many readers and so much attention? Clearly, the fantasies animating the novel struck a deep chord, resonating widely, illuminating and shaping cultural fissures from an emerging right-wing secular capitalist or "libertarian" point of view.

The plot of *Atlas Shrugged* is basically a moral fable that reverses the moral premises of early twentieth-century socialism and of midcentury welfare state liberalism. The novel represents the "producers" who own and run industrial capitalism as sexy, gorgeous, brilliant, and thoroughly admirable heroes, as contrasted with the flabby, unattractive, incompetent, unproductive moochers and state-backed bureaucratic looters, parasites, and thugs. Originally titled "The Strike," the novel outlines the impact on the world when the producers—the creators and innovators of industry, science, and intellectual life—rather than the unionized workers—withdraw their labor. The "engine of the world" progressively collapses, until the lights literally go out in New York City in a scene of desperate chaos. The producers have withdrawn to the hero John Galt's Gulch, planning to return once the world collapses without them.

This overall framework for the plot is structured in time and space with reference to notions of civilizational progress, American exceptionalism, a nineteenth-century version of idealized industrial capitalism, a hierarchy of ability and capacity, and an account of the destructive, regressive impact of "collectivism," both social and familial.

The civilizational theme echoes the one that shapes *Anthem*. The world of the contemporary United States, the setting of *Atlas Shrugged*, has fallen heavily under the sway of collectivist government regulation. The result is civilizational regression, a slide backward to more "savage," "tribal," "primitive," or "Asiatic" modes of life.[12] This is especially tragic for the United States, the only country born into true freedom, from the vision of the Founding Fathers to the apotheosis of so-far existing capitalism—the nineteenth-century form of supposedly individualist, entrepreneurial, relatively unregulated dynamic industrial growth. The fall from this period of political and economic grace begins with the first successes of socialism, in the Bolshevik revolution, and generates civilizational stasis and regression via the mixed economy of the welfare state. The utopia waiting in the wings, Galt's Gulch, is presented as a strange space-time warp. The life of the Gulch, which is located in Colorado, appears primarily as an idealized version of the American West. The producers make their livings as farmers, bakers, mechanics, and so forth—small business owners with homespun values of honesty and self-sufficiency—with no corporate offices or teams of corporate lawyers in sight. But high-tech inventions operate there as well, as indicators of the creative innovations that the producers contribute. Meanwhile, there is no sign of an indigenous population. The purity and nobility of the western setting depends on the erasure of histories of the violence of empire, slavery, and settler colonialism that brought these Europeans to this setting. The capitalism practiced in the Gulch is also free of detectable labor exploitation, and nearly free of any trace of reproductive labor or family life. Very few women are present there at all. One nameless baker is described as a mother by choice, and only one woman is named—Kay Ludlow, a glamorous actress.

The characters, starkly divided into good and evil, serve to illustrate various dimensions of stasis and decline, and the possibilities for regeneration ultimately waiting in Galt's Gulch. Beautiful and brilliant Dagny Taggart, the central heroine of the tale, runs Taggart Transcontinental under the incompetent authority of her brother James, who conspires and colludes with government officials to compensate for his own inadequacies. The romance plot of *Atlas Shrugged* is centered around her three affairs with dapper Francisco d'Anconia, a copper magnate; stalwart innovator Henry (Hank) Rearden, a steel manufacturer; and her vision of masculine perfection, John Galt, the mysterious engineer who leads the strike of the original title. The bulk of the plot follows the education of Dagny and Hank as they learn the moral lessons of reason and individualism and the necessity to decisively reject misguided altruism and collectivism.

Following along, the reader becomes witness to large-scale destruction and misery, to train wrecks and explosions and economic and technical failures that pile up as the producers secede from their roles in the world. The disaster-riven United States resembles Rand's view of Russia from the Crimea to Petrograd during the 1920s: the Bolsheviks and their collaborators in *We the Living* and the bureaucrats and sellouts of *Atlas Shrugged* are close kin. As Dagny and Hank come to learn that they will only be contributing to the evil of collectivism if they do not withdraw to the Gulch, the reader is led to welcome the destruction as deserved. The producers are created by the author as vehicles for admiration and aspiration, based on an exalted identification with moral, mental, and physical perfection. The moochers and looters are offered as targets for contempt, resentment, and finally indifference to their well-deserved fate.

Rand peppers the novel with long-winded speeches, didactic inductions into her philosophy. The central pedagogical moments include speeches on the meaning of money, the disastrous impact of collectivist economics, the sixty-page script of a radio speech by John Galt outlining his philosophy, and a surprising speech on the morality of sex—all designed to turn common understandings upside down.

Francisco d'Anconia's money speech reverses the common maxim "Money is the root of all evil" to argue that money is the root of all good. Money, when properly aligned with the gold standard, is the means to store tradeable "value" in a world of free trade and free markets. Without it there is only the barrel of a gun. Another speech attacks the Marxist maxim "From each according to his ability, to each according to his need." The narrator, telling the story of the rise and fall of the Twentieth Century Motor Company, describes the perverse incentives that destroy the whole company when it becomes a cooperative enterprise—workers minimize their abilities and maximize their stated needs, everyone becomes a conniving malingerer, and things fall apart:

> The shiftless and irresponsible had a field day of it. They bred babies, they got girls into trouble, they dragged in every worthless relative they had from all over the country, every unmarried pregnant sister, for an extra "disability allowance," they got more sicknesses than any doctor could disapprove, they ruined their clothing, their furniture, their homes—what the hell, "the family" was paying for it![13]

The sixty pages that are John Galt's radio script took Rand nearly two years to write. In a tone of supremely confident authority, and with seemingly endless repetitive detail, it lays out her logical elaborations from her rendering of the philosophy of Aristotle, through the supreme value of reason, to the morality of individualism and the superiority of capitalism. The lessons for the student/reader are: reason is superior to mysticism/religion, egoism is a truer morality than altruism, and individualism leads upward and forward via capitalism, while collectivism leads down and back to socialist barbarism. When her editor at Random House, Bennett Cerf, asked her to cut the speech, she notoriously replied, "Would you cut the Bible?"[14]

As reviewers pointed out, *Atlas Shrugged* is not subtle. It is heavy-handed, hectoring, relentless. But it is also iconoclastic, sometimes surprising, and even occasionally funny. While most of the political points hammered into readers repeatedly through the novel are variations on familiar themes in twentieth-century right-wing "free market" politics, Rand really veers off the safe path rather dramatically on the issues of God and sex. Her adamant atheism alienated many otherwise enthusiastic conservative fans. Her treatment of sex was surprising and confusing to many readers, though no doubt delightful and encouraging to some others.

Francisco d'Anconia's speech on the morality of sex, delivered in conversation with Hank Rearden, argues for the positive value of (presumptively hetero) sexual joy. Sexual desire, he insists, reflects the highest human values. D'Anconia enlightens Rearden, who is married to a woman who beats him down with guilt and obligation, by expounding the view that his adulterous desire for Dagny, the "highest" type of woman, reflects the proper rule of reason in matters sexual. Dagny's successive affairs with d'Anconia, Rearden, and Galt are presented as high-minded as well as thrilling. And in romance fantasy mode, none of the men are resentful or antagonistic as she moves on from one to the other. The relations among them, producers all, are infused with homoerotic mutual admiration, as they all understand perfectly that the others will of course desire Dagny.

Rand's fiction is rife with romantic triangles and quadrangles, with adultery and divorce, with homoerotic bonds among a heroine's multiple lovers (though homoeroticism among women is unimaginable in the Randian fictional universe). There is no birth control or abortion, few children, virtually no housework. The sex scenes feature conquest and eroticized physical struggle as powerful women submit to dominant men. But they do not then cling, depend, or nag—only the weak and the wives do that. And the romances emphatically do not end in marriage. These are fantasies for the New Woman that cut in multiple directions. Aspirational creative and professional freedom, circumscribed within a context of consensual, ecstatic sexual submission to heroic men, is available to the superior single woman producer. All the other women are either nagging parasites or starving primitives and incompetents.

As *The Fountainhead* reflects Rand's view of 1920s and '30s Hollywood, so *Atlas Shrugged* constitutes her brief against the New Deal and the emerging welfare state of the '40s and '50s. Her satiric skills and flashes of humor appear primarily in her portraits of state bureaucrats with names like Wesley Mouch, who push ridiculous legislation like the Anti–Dog-Eat-Dog Bill, while scheming for power like classic comic villains. The corporate businessmen who collaborate with the bureaucrats are equally evil—incompetent and resentful of the ability of others. Included among these are the families of heroic Titans like Hank Rearden and Dagny Taggart; mothers, siblings, and wives function as burdens and barriers.

Along with academic studies such as David Riesman, Nathan Glazer, and Reuel Denney's *The Lonely Crowd* (1950) and William Whyte's *The Organization Man* (1956), and fiction like Sloan Wilson's novel *The Man in the Gray Flannel Suit* (1955), *Atlas Shrugged* critiqued the "other directed" managers of mid-twentieth-century corporate capitalism and the regulatory welfare state.[15] But rather than a complex depiction and analysis, the novel provides a dramatically moralized landscape valorizing rugged individualism over all cooperative or collaborative values, at work or at home. This scenario repelled many critics, but by alternating bitter with hilarious depictions it also expressed widely shared frustrations with numbing, constraining bureaucratic corporate culture and parallel familial restraints.

Atlas Shrugged generally rallied the laissez-faire capitalist troops against the socialists, liberals, and religious conservatives. But it also appealed in complicated and contradictory ways across many other battle lines. As Judith Wilt has noted, the selfless devotion to the needs of others and the binding obligations to family that Rand so strenuously attacks and lampoons were values applied with special force to the lives of women. If most other major themes are bracketed, the novel can be read as a furious attack on normative femininity.[16] The homoerotic relations of the heroes have generated numerous queer "fan fiction" style appropriations that often ignore or revise the novel's broader political framework. And as Melissa Jane Hardie argues, the starkly dramatic, highly stylized, melodramatically moralized characterizations offer themselves for camp readings that twist and reverse Rand's preferred meanings.[17]

After the novel's 1957 publication, Rand's sky-high expectations were smashed. For a philosopher who valorized independence from the approval of others, she reacted horribly to the dearth of prominent defenders. "John Galt wouldn't feel like this," she complained to the Brandens as her depression deepened—probably also fueled by withdrawal from amphetamines.[18] For years after, she remained withdrawn and bitter as Nathaniel and Barbara Branden took over the propagation of the faith.

Drawing on Rand's fan mail for addresses, Nathaniel Branden put together a mailing list to advertise a new series of lectures, "The Basic Principles of Objectivism," in 1958. This first series was successful enough to be repeated twice a year as new series were added: Barbara Branden on the principles of efficient thinking, economist and Collective member Alan Greenspan on the economics of a free society, Ayn Rand herself on romantic realist fiction writing, and a second series that Nathaniel Branden may soon have come to regret, "The Principles of Romantic Love." These lecture series coalesced into the Nathaniel Branden Institute in 1961, a full-fledged educational enterprise that offered tapes of the lectures, with outposts in major cities from Philadelphia to Chicago and Los Angeles. The New

York center meanwhile expanded into a variegated social world that offered sports teams, movie and book clubs, and an annual ball. The *Objectivist Newsletter* began circulating in 1962, the same year that Nathaniel and Barbara Branden published a small biographical and philosophical volume designed to spread the word, *Who Is Ayn Rand?*[19] During the years of Rand's depressed withdrawal, the Brandens turned the by now very famous novelist into the fountainhead of an organized movement that registered 3,500 students in fifty cities at its peak in 1967.

The lecture courses and the *Objectivist Newsletter* initially boosted Rand's reputation, but soon rumors began circulating about a rigidly authoritarian personality cult at NBI and the Collective, at the center of organized Objectivism. In 1961, *Newsweek* compared Rand to evangelist Aimee Semple McPherson in her power to "hypnotize a live audience," and the *Saturday Evening Post* published a profile titled "The Curious Cult of Ayn Rand."[20] These news stories reported that NBI students were required not only to read *Atlas Shrugged,* but also to affirm their agreement with John Galt's speech. Anarchist libertarian Murray Rothbard fell in and out with Rand more than once, later describing "the Ayn Rand cult" in his usual purple prose style as comparable to the cults of Hitler, Mussolini, Trotsky, and Mao.[21] Psychologist Albert Ellis, founder of rational emotive behavior therapy, called Objectivism a religion and diagnosed Rand as a manic-depressive narcissist and a "fucking baby."[22] Rand seemed able to bring out the hothead in these devotees of reason.

Nathaniel Branden later admitted his central role in creating an atmosphere of judgment in which adherence to Rand's views was enforced with inquisitions and purges. In his 1986 memoir, *Judgment Day: My Years with Ayn Rand,* he listed the premises transmitted to students at NBI during the 1960s:

- Ayn Rand is the greatest human being who has ever lived.

- *Atlas Shrugged* is the greatest human achievement in the history of the world.

- Ayn Rand, by virtue of her philosophical genius, is the supreme arbiter in any issue pertaining to what is rational, moral, or appropriate to man's life on earth.

- Once one is acquainted with Ayn Rand and her work, the measure of one's virtue is intrinsically tied to the position that one takes regarding her and her work.

- No one who does not admire what Ayn Rand admires and condemns what Ayn Rand condemns can be a good Objectivist. No one who disagrees with Ayn Rand on any fundamental issue can be a fully consistent individual.

- Because Ayn Rand has designated Nathaniel Branden as her "intellectual heir" and has repeatedly proclaimed him to be an ideal exponent of her philosophy, he is to be accorded only marginally less reverence than Ayn Rand herself.

- It is best not to say most of these things explicitly (excepting, perhaps, the first two items). One must always maintain that one arrives at one's beliefs solely by reason.[23]

But as she emerged from the depths of her post-*Atlas* depression, Rand also began to develop a public role beyond the Collective, NBI, and Objectivist circles. She gave the lecture "Faith and Force: The Destroyers of the Modern World" at Yale, Princeton, Columbia, and Brooklyn College during 1960 and began appearing annually at the Ford Hall Forum at Northeastern University in Boston—an April event often called "Objectivist Easter."[24] The first of many Ayn Rand campus clubs formed at Brooklyn College as she developed a reputation as a provocative speaker and a right-wing icon in cape and dollar-sign pin with cigarette holder. Her campus lectures were popular and crowded, but she gained her widest audiences via a Mike Wallace interview broadcast in 1959 and three appearances on *The Tonight Show with Johnny Carson* in 1967—before a television audience of fifty million. Rand's television appearances were followed by record mail, nearly all positive. This surprised at least one producer on the Mike Wallace show, who noted that other media treated her as a "leper" and "the Antichrist."[25] The very respectful 1964 interview by Alvin Toffler in *Playboy* also exposed Rand and her philosophy to a mainstream audience, contributing to her highly polarizing reputation as either a sage or a nut job.[26]

Rand attracted college and television audiences with her pointed attacks on altruism and religion and passionate defenses of unregulated capitalism, both of which cut against the grain of popular opinion during the early 1960s. But she also appealed to many with her opposition to the Vietnam War, the draft, and the legal ban on abortion—positions that often surprised her interlocutors. She veered substantially from consensus liberalism and emerging New Left politics, but also from mainstream conservatism with the less familiar right-wing libertarian bent of her arguments.

As Ayn Rand moved slowly from the margins toward the center of mainstream visibility, she was carried along with the incoming tide of advocacy for laissez-faire capitalism. Barry Goldwater's 1964 campaign for president against Lyndon Baines Johnson served as a kind of weathervane. His 1960 book *The Conscience of a Conservative* introduced the thinking of laissez-faire economists Ludwig von Mises and Friedrich Hayek to a broader conservative audience, and by 1963 he had attracted the support of a cadre of outsiders to electoral politics—including advisors Milton Friedman and William F. Buckley—who elevated him to the Republican Party nomination. Ayn Rand, who had excoriated

John F. Kennedy as a "high class beatnik," was pleased to endorse Goldwater and correspond with him, though she was ultimately disappointed by his inconsistencies, and especially by his embrace of religion. His crushing defeat exposed the limited inroads of the antiunion, anti–welfare state business activists who were his primary supporters. But his campaign laid the basis for decades of more successful inroads to come as militant liberalism's supporters gained significant ground over the next two decades.[27]

Rand's contradictory public reputation, based on her image as both a cult leader and a popular public speaker, exploded and crashed in 1968. She never truly recovered, personally or publicly. The reasons were kept under wraps. Objectivist circles and the wider public knew only that Rand split with the Brandens, NBI dissolved, and Objectivism fractured and declined. In May 1968, Rand published a vague attack on her close associates in the *Objectivist Newsletter* titled "To Whom It May Concern," alleging unspecified personal immorality and financial improprieties (wholly invented). The Brandens seized the mailing list and sent out an equally vague reply in a letter to subscribers, "In Answer to Ayn Rand."[28] Confusion reigned. One thing seemed clear: emotion had brought down the house of reason.

The details emerged with books by each Branden, one in 1986—Barbara Branden's *The Passion of Ayn Rand* (made into a movie in 1999 starring Helen Mirren in the title role)—and the other in 1989—Nathaniel Branden's *Judgment Day: My Years with Ayn Rand*. The Brandens provided somewhat different versions of the sordid tale of Rand's affair with Nathaniel, undertaken with permission of both spouses, and its end with the revelation of Nathaniel's ongoing four-year secret relationship with a third woman, actress and Objectivist student Patrecia Scott (born Gullison, professional name Wynand). Although Rand had been celibate during her depression, and Branden had resisted restarting their affair for years after her revival, the revelation of the affair with Scott sent Rand over the edge from scorched-earth rage into personal desolation. In her view, Nathaniel had proved himself a fraud and a failure as an Objectivist, not only because of his lies, but because of his choice of an "inferior value" in his sexual life. The entire edifice of Ayn Rand's idealized romantic sexual philosophy came crashing down, as the man she called a genius and hero, her anointed heir, rejected her and lied to *her* about his sex life. There was no room for such weakness and failure in her philosophy. She accused Branden of having taken away "this earth." Barbara Branden simply summarized, "Ayn wants you dead."[29]

Though devastated and diminished, Ayn Rand did not disappear from public view. During the 1960s she developed four distinct voices that carried her influence forward. The first was found in her massively popular novels, which circulated cultural fantasies of individualist American Titans who struggle and triumph over the burdens and barriers imposed by the weak and corrupt tribalists and collectivists who want only to confiscate their wealth and sap their strength. This rewriting of the Horatio Alger story of up-by-the-bootstraps achievement was composed through and over the story of European civilizational progress against the savage and primitive tribes of the Americas, Asia, and Africa. American exceptionalism is overt in Rand's fictional narratives; civilizational triumph provides a baseline framework. Moral evaluations are embedded in hierarchies of ability, capacity, and beauty. The stark racial hierarchies of these frameworks are obscured by the fact that all the major characters are white.[30]

The fantasy worlds of *The Fountainhead* and *Atlas Shrugged* reproduce deep, widely shared cultural narratives. That these narratives reflect the dominant view of relatively privileged Americans of European descent is seen in the fact that the fan base for Ayn Rand's fiction, though mixed by gender and sexual identity, is predominantly composed of white members of the aspiring professional, managerial, creative, and business classes.

The second public voice of Ayn Rand during the 1960s was represented by her campus lecture and media persona. This Rand was provocative but personable, pedagogical, and sometimes funny. The published lectures address a confused and questioning "you" in clear and teacherly prose.[31] The *Playboy* interview and the televised appearances present Rand's answers to challenging questions in clear, confident, measured, but blunt language.

> MIKE WALLACE: And then if a man is weak, or a woman is weak, then she is beyond, he is beyond love?
>
> AYN RAND: He certainly does not deserve it, he certainly is beyond. He can always correct it. Man has free will. If a man wants love he should correct his weaknesses, or his flaws, and he may deserve it. But he cannot expect the unearned, neither in love, nor in money, neither in matter, nor spirit.[32]

This provocative but engaging public presence starkly contrasted with Rand's third voice as an authoritarian cult leader. This voice circulated secondhand, through an accumulating pile of critical and satirical news reports and memoirs, capped by descriptions like Jerome Tuccille's in his 1971 comic tale of life in Objectivism, *It Usually Begins with Ayn Rand:*

> ... Curiously enough, for a woman who started out as a champion of the independent mind, she began to consider her own ideas as natural corollaries of truth and objectivity.
>
> "Objective reality" was what Rand said it was.
>
> "Morality" was conformity to the ethic of Ayn Rand.

"Rationality" was synonymous with the thinking of Ayn Rand....

... *Atlas Shrugged* ... quickly became a kind of New Marxism of the Right.[33]

This severe voice was echoed in writing in the *Objectivist Newsletter* (1962–1965, later the *Objectivist* magazine, 1966–1971, and then the *Ayn Rand Letter,* 1971–1976). Selected essays from the newsletter were reproduced in a series of books during the 1960s and early '70s. The first of these, *For the New Intellectual,* reprinted excerpts from her novels prefaced by an extended essay of breathtaking scope. The essay laid out the theory of history and philosophy that underpins her novels: From a promising beginning among the Greeks, represented by Aristotle rather than Plato, man's potential for reason and achievement took a deep dive during the Dark Ages, when the Witch Doctor (religious mystics) and Attila (strongmen who rule by force) held sway over savage, primitive barbarian hordes whose tribal practices included human sacrifice. The Renaissance brought back Aristotle and the rise of European reason. In America, rational morality powered the rise of capitalism, which by the nineteenth century reached its purest (but still not really pure) form. In the twentieth century, the rise of socialist collectivism and the influence of Immanuel Kant ruined everything. The intellectuals are primarily to blame for ideas that support the "mixed economy" responsible for the political and economic ills of the twentieth century.[34]

This sounds cartoonish. It is. Its finger-in-your-eye tone and absurdly reductive account of both history and philosophy clashed with Rand's much more careful and appealing public-speaking persona. As Gore Vidal commented in his 1961 review of *For the New Intellectual,*

Miss Rand now tells us that what we have thought was right is really wrong. The lesson should have read: One for one and none for all.... Ayn Rand's philosophy is nearly perfect in its immorality, which makes the size of her audience all the more ominous and systematic as we enter a curious new phase in our society. Moral values are in flux. The muddy depths are being stirred by new monsters and witches from the deep. Trolls walk the American night.[35]

Subsequent volumes, including *The Virtue of Selfishness* (1961) and *Capitalism: The Unknown Ideal* (1966), were composed of essays by Rand, Nathaniel Branden, Alan Greenspan, and Robert Hessen primarily devoted to the defense of property rights, the central plank of the political platform of these "radicals for capitalism." But each also included an essay a bit off that track.

In "Racism," Rand criticizes racism as the "lowest most crudely primitive form of collectivism" and expresses her support for the agenda of the civil rights movement, to the extent that it opposes government-backed discrimination.[36] She goes on to attack the 1964 Civil Rights Act in the same terms that Barry Goldwater did, as a violation of property rights. Arguing that "private" discrimination is a moral, not a legal crime, she proceeds to defend "color blind" government policies over any move toward collective rights or "quotas"—which she associates with the anti-Semitic quota ceilings of czarist Russia. When paired with her opening rant in *For the New Intellectual,* this exposition of "color blind" racial policies illuminates the ways racial hierarchies persisted even as American apartheid laws were dismantled. For Rand, the erasure of indigenous people, restrictions on immigration from more "primitive" parts of the world, and the persistence of sharp racial inequality in the "private" economic and social spheres were part and parcel of her system of rational morality, even as she opposed state-imposed racial (and sex) discrimination.

In "The Wreckage of the Consensus," delivered as a lecture in 1967 and added to the revised paperback edition of *Capitalism: The Unknown Ideal* (1967), Rand begins to track the breakdown of the welfare-state consensus of the postwar period. She wonders what alternative might emerge, and points to then–governor of California Ronald Reagan's famous speech nominating Barry Goldwater in 1964 as a promising new direction for electoral politics—a new direction her own influence helped shape.[37]

The last two volumes of Rand's writing published during her lifetime were starkly contrasting. *The Romantic Manifesto* (1971) included her defense of romanticism, her attacks on naturalism and modernism, and her extended definition of the notion of "sense of life." *The New Left: The Anti-Industrial Revolution* (1971, later retitled as *Return of the Primitive*) reads like a series of screeds on contemporary issues scrawled by a cranky recluse whose only sources of information are popular news magazines and television reports. The essays are unified by her critique of the New Left, as a manifestation of primitive regression. They include complaints about "hippies" and "beatniks," especially at Woodstock in 1969—dirty descendants of Dionysius, as compared with the Apollonians (including herself) in attendance at the launch of Apollo 11 that same year. She takes a swipe at "Women's Lib" as a bunch of unattractive women (like her character in *We the Living*, Comrade Sonia) who are demanding "special rights" rather than legitimate "equal rights." She focuses especially on the movement for ecology, which she describes as at the core of an anti-industrial revolution. In "The Age of Envy" she summarizes her view of the threats to Western civilization, as represented by the primitive, the disabled, and the stupid:

Why is Western civilization admonished to admire primitive cultures? Because they are *not* admirable. Why is primitive man exhorted to ignore Western achievements? Because they *are*. Why is the self-expression of a retarded adolescent to be nurtured and acclaimed? Because he has nothing to express. Why is the self-expression of a genius to be impeded and ignored? Because he *has*.[38]

Ayn Rand's fourth public voice was a muted one. Off and on during the 1960s and '70s she published explications of her philosophy in her most academic prose, including sections of *Introduction to Objectivist Epistemology* in the *Objectivist Newsletter;* the book appeared in 1979.

During the 1970s, as the postwar consensus continued to unravel, the nascent, fractious political right in the United States transformed. Old-school free marketeers, anticommunist activists, and traditional conservatives were joined and ultimately superseded by an emerging conservative youth movement, an expanding libertarian movement, a mobilizing religious right, and a hard-edged form of law-and-order populism reflected by the election of Richard Nixon in 1968. An upsurge in business activism joined with elements of these libertarian and conservative strains to usher in the rise and dominance of neoliberalism by the 1980s election of Ronald Reagan to the U.S. presidency. Ayn Rand's Mean Girl influence, her promotion of optimistic cruelty, was a vital element of this new hegemony.

FOUR

"I Found a Flaw"

In 2018, tech writer Douglas Rushkoff met with a handful of hedge fund billionaires to talk about the future of technology. But they were actually most interested in enlisting his help in filling in the details for their vision of the dystopian future—or rather, for their own high-tech vision of a Galt's Gulch–style escape from it. Writing in *Medium*, Rushkoff described their questions about future apocalypse:

> The Event... was their euphemism for the environmental collapse, social unrest, nuclear explosion, unstoppable virus, or Mr. Robot hack that takes everything down.
>
> ... They knew armed guards would be required to protect their compounds from the angry mobs. But how would they pay the guards once money was worthless? What would stop the guards from choosing their own leader? The billionaires considered using special combination locks on the food supply that only they knew. Or making guards wear disciplinary collars of some kind in return for their survival. Or maybe building robots to serve as guards and workers—if that technology could be developed in time.

… They were preparing for a digital future that had a whole lot less to do with making the future a better place than it did with … insulating themselves from a very real and present danger of climate change, rising sea levels, mass migrations, global pandemics, nativist panic, and resource depletion. …

Asking these sorts of questions, while philosophically entertaining, is a poor substitute for wrestling with the real moral quandaries associated with unbridled technological development in the name of corporate capitalism.[1]

These unnamed hedge fund honchos may have read *Atlas Shrugged,* but even those who hadn't would likely have been familiar with John Galt and the producers' utopia he created far from the collapsing world. By 2018 Ayn Rand and her novels had become widespread cultural reference points among wealthy bankers, CEOs, tech moguls, and right-wing politicians.

Rand's philosophy had its roots in nineteenth-century classical liberalism and in her impassioned rejection of socialism and the welfare state in the twentieth century. Her anti-statist, pro– "free market" stances went on to shape the politics of what came to be called libertarianism, or sometimes anarcho-capitalism, during a period of rapid expansion in the 1970s. The rise of neoliberalism has a parallel history, and much overlap with libertarianism—but these formations nonetheless have distinct trajectories. Rand's influence floats over all of them as a guiding spirit for the sense of energized aspiration and the advocacy of inequality and cruelty that shaped their worldviews. By the 2018 meeting with Rushkoff, however, the billionaires could no longer be called optimistic. Their plans differ from Galt's intention to return to save the world; the contemporary billionaires are only hoping to escape and survive the ruin—in high-tech style.

Ayn Rand bitterly rejected libertarians as right-wing "hippies" in the 1970s, but her views and those of her Objectivist followers melded substantially with the emerging libertarian movement. Young enthusiasts were joining older libertarian warhorses to create new organizations, publications, and institutions. Libertarian "rads" split from conservative "trads" in Young Americans for Freedom in 1969 and went on to help found the new Libertarian Party in 1971. The *New York Times Magazine* featured a major story that January tracking these developments: "The New Right Credo—Libertarianism."[2]

During the 1970s, chapters of organizations like the Society for Individual Liberty proliferated along with popular publications such as *Reason* magazine. A yearly libertarian studies conference, the Center for Libertarian Studies, and the *Journal of Libertarian Studies* established a foothold in academic life. The influential Cato Institute was originally opened as the libertarian Charles Koch Foundation in 1974. The libertarians, who clashed on a wide range of issues, ranged from countercultural left libertarians, to pragmatic advocates of a minimal state ("minarchists"), to a fiery right wing of adamantly anti-state anarcho-capitalists. Objectivists were prominent in all of their activities; reading Rand's novels became a rite of passage for many. Rand herself disapproved of the lack of philosophical discipline among the motley crew of young libertarians, however, announcing that "if such hippies hope to make me their Marcuse, it will not work."[3]

Rand just got crankier and crankier as the years went by. She continued giving a few public lectures and publishing short essays on current events. She was interviewed by Phil Donahue; she began work on a television script for *Atlas Shrugged* that was never produced. Her health began a long decline when her lifetime of heavy smoking resulted in a diagnosis of lung cancer in 1974 (though she denied the connection between smoking and cancer to the end). The death of Frank O'Connor in 1979 hit her hard. Barbara Branden and Nathaniel Branden's third wife both visited her in 1981, hoping to establish friendly contact with them and with Nathaniel, but she ultimately rejected their overtures. She alienated nearly all her friends and colleagues one by one over the years, leaving only her heir, philosopher Leonard Peikoff, and a few others at her death in 1982. Objectivism meanwhile lived on—both in the loyal band of followers associated with the Ayn Rand Institute (founded by Peikoff in 1985) and in those who split off, feeling freer to branch out into more heterodox formations after Rand's death.[4]

As libertarianism spread and Rand withdrew, a new political economic formation began to take center stage. Becoming organized in the late 1940s with the establishment of the Mont Pelerin Society (MPS), neoliberal thinkers accumulated power and influence over the decades, to the point of seizing state power by the 1980s. Hard to define and largely hidden from view in the early years (the term was first used in 1925), neoliberalism was just one thread in the wild and woolly fabric of right-wing politics in the United States and Europe. The founding of the MPS helped define it as a distinct tendency among the classical liberals, Burkean traditionalists, libertarians, anarcho-capitalists, religious conservatives, right-wing racial nationalists, and fascists. Organized primarily by economist Friedrich Hayek, the more than one thousand economists, journalists, policy makers, and other thinkers who eventually gathered under the MPS umbrella formed what Philip Mirowski has called a "Neoliberal Thought Collective"—an intellectual/political intervention that eventually defined a new era of capitalism.[5]

Although neoliberalism was never monolithic, the neoliberal project was focused on the need to develop a "new liberalism" to replace the outmoded concepts of nineteenth-century classical liberalism. The primary goal—remaking the infrastructure of states and markets in the post–Great Depression and post–World War II world—did not comport with the "laissez-faire" capitalism of an earlier era. The neoliberals set out to retool the state in relation to the market values of property rights and corporate hegemony. While their public propaganda efforts emphasized the keyword *freedom* and linked so-called free markets with free minds, they set out via activist interventions in state policy to create a decidedly planned version of "laissez-faire."[6]

This gap between the public face and the relatively hidden political planning of neoliberals has been described by David Harvey as a contrast between the utopian theory of neoliberal freedom and the practical class project of installing oligarchical elites at the center of economic and state power.[7] Neoliberalism is often misunderstood through its utopian propaganda as an effort to shrink the state and free the natural operations of "the market." But neoliberals redirect state efforts rather than diminish them. The "Neoliberal Thought Collective," combined with the various allied political policy centers of neoliberal action, might be understood as a global anti-left social movement. Nancy MacLean has traced the planning of various neoliberal forces—through foundations, think tanks, research centers and private funders—to create new barriers to democratic decision-making, in the interests of corporate power. She describes how Charles Koch was introduced to the thinking of Russian revolutionary Vladimir Lenin by anarcho-capitalist Murray Rothbard. Always learning from the left, Koch drew from Lenin's thinking to develop plans for well-trained cadres that could prevail over a majority in the political arena. (Today, Lenin's adherents on the right include former Breitbart editor and Trump advisor Steve Bannon.)[8]

Neoliberalism was initially centered in Europe and the United States, focused on attacking the influence of John Maynard Keynes and the welfare states his thinking helped establish. The point of neoliberal effort was to free capitalism from the "mixed economies" that emphasized limited forms of social security, financial regulation, empowerment of labor, social services, and public ownership. The slow-motion collapse of the Fordist economies of secure employment, with relatively high wages and benefits, opened the door to new macroeconomic, monetary, and fiscal policies advocated by the Neoliberal Thought Collective—including privatization of public services, re-regulation of corporate operations, and erosion of consumer and workplace protections.

Though this process of "neoliberalization" was represented as race blind, many of the ideas and policies evolved out of resistance to the civil rights movement in the United States, via what Nancy MacLean has called "property supremacy." Opposition to the Civil Rights Act of 1964 was often articulated as a defense of private property against government interference, rather than as racial animus. Claims were made for the freedom of private property owners to discriminate against anyone for any reason. During "massive resistance" to civil rights in the U.S. South, the creation of private "segregation academies" sometimes displaced support for public schools—a model for later neoliberal strategies for privatization of education. But the critique of government institutions did not extend to legislative efforts to suppress voting rights and "law and order" police suppression of political dissent. In those circumstances state action was required to defend property rights from democracy as well as disorder.[9]

In 1980, neoliberal politicians Ronald Reagan and Margaret Thatcher ascended to become heads of state in the United States and United Kingdom. In subsequent years, neoliberal politics and policies moved social democratic parties unevenly toward neoliberalism all across Europe. During the 1990s the neoliberal Washington Consensus took form, and the 1992 Maastricht Treaty founded the European Union on neoliberal principles.

But the neoliberal political project was pursued far beyond Europe and the United States. Fundamentally, neoliberalism was a global extension of European colonialism on the nonterritorial U.S. imperial model. During the mid–twentieth century, former colonies throughout the Global South declared independence. New postcolonial states in Asia, Africa, the Middle East, Latin America, and the Caribbean instituted a range of strategies to establish growth and autonomy: restrictions on foreign investment, replacement of imports with local production, the redistribution of land, and the launching of ambitious public projects and social supports. Global neoliberalism was engineered to erode those strategies.

Violence was a central method for the imposition of neoliberalism in the Global South. The 1973 coup in Chile and the 2003 invasion of Iraq were both followed by foreign investment, resource extraction, and privatization of public assets. But the primary means for reestablishing the economic exploitation and political domination that are key to racial capitalism was the trap of debt.

Through lending to impoverished postcolonial states, financial institutions based in the Global North (especially the International Monetary Fund) were able to impose "structural adjustment" requirements on debtor nations in the South. After the 1989 fall of the USSR, neoliberalism entwined with various forms of postsocialist governance in states of the former Russian empire. Neoliberal policies also reshaped late twentieth-century China.

More recently, forms of authoritarian neoliberalism mixed with right-wing populism are in ascendance in India, the Philippines, and elsewhere.[10]

Neoliberal influence has been culturally deep as well as geographically wide. Drawing on the work of Michel Foucault, a multidisciplinary group of scholars have described the reach of neoliberal modes of governance into the conduct of everyday life. To counter the solidarity economies and social cooperation of organized workers, public-spirited officials, and professionals, neoliberals have promoted the Entrepreneurial Self who competes in the Aspiration Society. Everyone invests in their own personal and familial human capital, and all are responsible for their own risk-taking and rewards, or the lack of them. According to these conceptions, the poor are not a class, but a collection of individual failures. The rich are not exploitive parasites on the labor of the majority, but the very source of wealth and a boon to society. Except that, as Margaret Thatcher noted, "society" as such does not exist. The social is the context for individual striving. It is also the scene of the Neoliberal Theater of Cruelty, through which feelings of resentment, fear, anger, and loathing are enacted against the weak, who are a drain on the worthy. Cracking down on welfare "cheats," "illegal" immigrants, and homeless "vagrants" can become a form of public satisfaction.

But the everyday life of neoliberalism—a template for living as well as governance—is not always so dramatic. Neoliberal cultures are multiple, and include "soft" multicultural, inclusive, and self-help–infused versions. Bill Clinton and Tony Blair, Barack Obama and Angela Merkel represent a range of softer versions. They have steered clear of the open-air theater of cruelty approach, while also busying themselves with stripping away the social safety net and backing the investor class—Bill Clinton abolished "welfare as we know it," and Obama put Wall Street bankers in charge of dealing with the economic crisis in 2008. Under both soft and hard versions, everyday life is infused with the nuts-and-bolts preoccupations of neoliberalism more than with the spectacular—arranging medical care, purchasing insurance, checking credit scores, going to the gym, paying student loans, worrying about housing costs, getting kids into schools. The reorganization of the infrastructure of political and economic life has reached deeply into daily living, erasing many of the boundaries between "the market" and the body, the family, emotional life. Everyday preoccupations in neoliberal times center on surviving a precarious employment landscape and investing in the skills and traits needed to keep moving—rather than on building the solidarity that might underwrite a broad remaking of political and economic infrastructure. As a bus stop advertisement for New York University recently put it, "I am the CEO of Me, Inc."[11]

Then in 2007 and 2008, it looked like it all might come tumbling down. The collapse of the subprime mortgage market in the United States reverberated through global financial institutions, then infected markets and industries well beyond banking and housing. Losses were deep and broad. Neoliberal strategies of privatization, deregulation (especially of finance), and minimization of social services lost support in the short run. But their supporters soon recovered their nerve and Zombie Neoliberalism stalked the land. As Fredric Jameson and others have argued, economics is a story more than a science. And the story the Neoliberal Thought Collective told in the wake of the 2008 economic crisis was: More and better neoliberalism is the cure for, not the cause of, economic crisis. More tax cuts, less regulation, intensified theaters of cruelty! In Philip Mirowski's phrasing, more "everyday sadism."[12] Those losing their homes are to blame for their bad mortgages; immigrants are to blame for citizens' job losses and precarity; everyone should be responsible for their own healthcare! And in an especially tricky twist, the groups calling for neoliberal remedies for neoliberal crises (like the Tea Party) posed as outsiders—Fight the Power! Identifying the power became the crux of the problem.[13]

During the decade since the crisis of 2008, politics have increasingly polarized in volatile ways around the world. The "center" of neoliberal consensus seems to be progressively collapsing, despite the strenuous efforts and significant successes of the Zombies. Left activism and right-wing mobilization have expanded rapidly. In this polarized landscape, Ayn Rand pops up as a kind of avatar of capitalist "freedom." From a figure admired largely on the margins of U.S. politics, she moved into the political center in the decades after 1980—or rather, the center moved toward her.

Ayn Rand's popularity has had four significant high points: (1) from the publication of *The Fountainhead* to the appearance of *Atlas Shrugged* (1943–1957); (2) among newly ascendant neoliberals during the 1980s; (3) among the new tech tycoons of Silicon Valley during the 1990s and after; and (4) during and after the 2008 crash. The link between the first two periods can be traced through the career of Alan Greenspan.

Greenspan became a regular at Rand's Collective meetings during the 1950s, accompanying his first wife, Joan Mitchell. At first quiet and circumspect, Greenspan slowly waded into debates with Rand—who called him the Undertaker. He was a math whiz, a logical positivist, a committed empiricist technocrat when he encountered Objectivism. But then, he explains in his memoir *The Age of Turbulence*, "Rand persuaded me to look at human beings, their values, how they work, what they do and why they do it, and how they think and why they think. This broadened my horizons far beyond the models of economics I'd learned.... She introduced me to a vast realm from which I'd shut myself off."[14]

His work and reputation as an economic consultant took off during the 1960s, when he delivered lectures at the Nathaniel Branden Institute and published in the *Objectivist.* In 1974, as neoliberal thinking began to move increasingly away from pure forms of libertarian philosophy and toward the project of reshaping state power, Greenspan moved into a new post on President Gerald Ford's Council of Economic Advisors (Rand and Frank O'Connor accompanied him to the swearing in). In his new location at the center of administrative power, he abandoned his advocacy of the gold standard and opposition to central banks. In 1987, he was appointed by President Reagan to be chairman of the Federal Reserve. From there until his retirement in 2006, Greenspan presided over the deregulation of the U.S.-based financial system.[15]

Alan Greenspan thus became one of the most important neoliberal policy makers in world history. His rise to this position required compromises and shifts from his earlier, purist Objectivist views. Rand herself clung tightly to her integrated, uncompromising philosophy. She was thus not exactly a neoliberal herself—she shunned the negotiations required to retool the economic and political infrastructure as neoliberals aspired to do. She remained a propagandist, an Objectivist purist, and a drama queen presiding over her fictional Theaters of Cruelty, providing templates, plot lines, and characters for the everyday fantasies of the neoliberal era. She promoted the Entrepreneurial Self, attacked solidarity and socialism, and posed as the ultimate rebel, the icon of capitalist freedom. In this, she stood alongside rather than within the neoliberal project. Her spirit certainly guided major neoliberal institutions and publications—including the Cato Institute (directed from 2012 to 2015 by Objectivist and Ayn Rand Institute board member John Allison) and *Reason* magazine (founded in 1968 to support the Randian project of "free minds and free markets").

Rand acolytes were spread throughout the world of business during the 1980s and '90s, but the tech gurus of Silicon Valley have been an especially rich source of Ayn Rand fandom. As Nick Bolton explains in a 2016 issue of *Vanity Fair,*

> Perhaps the most influential figure in the industry, after all, isn't Steve Jobs or Sheryl Sandberg, but rather Ayn Rand. Jobs's co-founder, Steve Wozniak, has suggested that *Atlas Shrugged* was one of Jobs's "guides in life." For a time, [Uber founder Travis] Kalanick's Twitter avatar featured the cover of *The Fountainhead.* [Paypal founder] Peter Thiel ... is also a self-described Rand devotee.
>
> At their core, Rand's philosophies suggest that it's O.K. to be selfish, greedy, and self-interested, especially in business, and that a win-at-all-costs mentality is just the price of changing the norms of society. As one start-up founder recently told me, "They should retitle her books *It's O.K. to Be a Sociopath!*" And yet most tech entrepreneurs and engineers appear to live by one of Rand's defining mantras: The question isn't who is going to let me; it's who is going to stop me.[16]

The Randian ethos of the heroic individual entrepreneur as alpha white male (and sometimes female) genius fits the self-mythologizing self-image of Silicon Valley tech startups particularly well.

It might have been expected that the bursting of the 1990s dot.com bubble and the early twenty-first-century financial crisis would have pulled the plug on some these hot-air balloons. Even Alan Greenspan admitted during a 2008 congressional hearing that, "Yes, I found a flaw" in the ideology underpinning his deregulating fervor as chair of the Federal Reserve.[17] But Ayn Rand rose with the Zombies after 2008, with a big sales surge for *Atlas Shrugged*. Tea Partiers and others saw the financial collapse and economic crisis as following the plotline of that novel. John Galt to the rescue meant ... time for more and better neoliberalism.

The election of Donald Trump in 2016 would seem on the surface to constitute a repudiation of Randism. Trump is in most ways a Rand villain—a businessman who relies on cronyism and manipulation of government, who advocates interference in so-called "free markets," who bullies big companies to do his bidding, who doesn't read. His personal and public corruption mirror her character sketches of sellouts and dirtbags. Trump draws from nationalism in his rhetoric and some of his policies, and panders to religious conservatives—both ideologies Rand found odious. Yet he praises *The Fountainhead:* "It relates to business, beauty, life and inner emotions. The book relates to ... everything."[18] His cabinet and donor lists are full of Rand fans.[19]

The question arises with the election of Trump and the success of far-right nationalism and populism around the world—are these still neoliberal times? Are the Zombies reinforcing their infrastructure and deepening their hold with policies like the U.S. tax cut bill, the appointment of neoliberal judges, the extended privatization of healthcare and education, the gutting of environmental regulations that businesses oppose? Or is neoliberalism collapsing? Are we seeing the rise of security states and fascist parties that might replace neoliberal hegemony with something new—something terrifying? Or might we see socialist organizing reach toward something more egalitarian and inclusive, something exciting?[20] The reign of the cruel optimism of Mean Girl Ayn

Rand is one barometer. Rand cannot be a presiding spirit for right-wing nationalism or for socialism. She is the avatar of capitalism, in its militant form as market liberalism. If neoliberalism crashes and burns in public acceptability, so does she.

What can we all do? Organize, of course, as so many on the global feminist, antiracist, anti-neoliberal left are now doing. But also, expose the cruelty at the heart of neoliberalism, and build on the social solidarity she worked so hard to discredit and destroy. Reject Ayn Rand. After all, she rejects you.

ACKNOWLEDGMENTS

My weird obsession with Ayn Rand began many years ago, shared in secret with Nan D. Hunter. Then the rest of the world seemed to catch up with me, as Ayn Rand's visage, novel titles, and characters appeared seemingly everywhere after 2008. So I finally decided to write about her, as a way to write about the sanctioned, even moralized greed of neoliberal racial capitalism.

This little book made sense to me as a contribution to the series *American Studies Now*—short, timely, accessible books for activists as well as students, coedited by Curtis Marez and me. I decided I wanted to contribute to my own series with a volume on neoliberalism, explained through a focus on Ayn Rand. Thanks to University of California Press editor Niels Hooper for encouraging both the series and this book, and to Curtis for conspiring with me. Thank you as well to Anna McCarthy, Janet Jakobsen, and Rod Ferguson for the thoughtful provocations and feedback. I am grateful to the whole field of American Studies, all my colleagues and students, for their collective devotion to scholarship as intellectual activism. I do not thank Kitty Gaga, who impeded my progress at every turn—but I do adore her.

NOTES

PREFACE

1. The wildly popular 2004 movie *Mean Girls,* written by Tina Fey, was based on Rosalind Wiseman, *Queen Bees and Wannabes* (New York: Three Rivers Press, 2002). See Richard Brody, "Why 'Mean Girls' Is a Classic," *New Yorker,* Apr. 30, 2014; and Esther Zuckerman, "Revisiting 'Mean Girls' with Rosalind Wiseman," *Wire,* Apr. 28, 2014. A Broadway musical version of the movie, also written by Fey, opened in 2017. The movie *Wall Street* (1987), featuring the character Gordon Gekko (portrayed by Michael Douglas), became an iconic representation of neoliberal greed.

2. Biographies, articles, and press reports all list the famous followers of Ayn Rand. See, for example, Gary Weiss, *Ayn Rand Nation: The Hidden Struggle for America's Soul* (New York: St. Martin's Press, 2012); Jenny Turner, "As Astonishing as Elvis," *London Review of Books,* Dec. 1, 2005; Sam Anderson, "Mrs. Logic," *New York Magazine,* Oct. 18, 2009; and Robert Reich, "Trump's Brand is Ayn Rand," *Nation of Change,* Mar. 6, 2018.

3. Art Carden, "What Ayn Rand's *Atlas Shrugged* Teaches Us about the Insufficiency of Good Intentions," *Forbes,* Apr. 23, 2018.

4. Jennifer Burns's description of Ayn Rand's fiction as the "ultimate gateway drug" to right-wing politics was quoted in nearly all the reviews and interviews surrounding the publication of her *Goddess of the Market: Ayn Rand and the American Right* (New York: Oxford University Press, 2009). See, for example, Linda Y. Li, "Atlas Drugged," *American Prospect*, Nov. 6, 2009; and "Stephen Colbert Interviews Author Jennifer Burns on Ayn Rand and the Republican Party," *Huffpost*, Aug. 30, 2012.

5. On the concept "structure of feeling," see Raymond Williams, *Marxism and Literature* (London: Oxford University Press, 1977), esp. 133.

6. Lauren Berlant, *Cruel Optimism* (Durham, NC: Duke University Press, 2011).

7. There are no studies of the readers and followers of Ayn Rand, though many commenters note that they appear to be overwhelmingly white young men and women of the middle classes. For a more extended effort to understand Rand's readers, see Claudia Franziska Brühwiler, "Pitiless Adolescents and Young Crusaders: Reimagining Ayn Rand's Readers," *Canadian Review of American Studies* 46, no. 1 (Spring 2016): 42–61.

8. Slavoj Žižek, "The Actuality of Ayn Rand," *Journal of Ayn Rand Studies* 3, no. 2 (2002): 215–227.

INTRODUCTION. "WHAT IS GOOD FOR ME IS RIGHT"

1. Jerome Tuccille, *It Usually Begins with Ayn Rand* (New York: Stein & Day, 1971), opening of "Part One: The Overview."

2. Richard H. Cantillon, *In Defense of the Fox: The Trial of William Edward Hickman* (Atlanta: Droke House/Hallux, 1972); James L. Neibaur, *Butterfly in the Rain: The 1927 Abduction and Murder of Marion Parker* (New York: Rowman & Littlefield, 2016).

3. Rand's plan for *The Little Street* receives extended discussion in her journals. The outline as it appears there is not entirely reliable, however. As Jennifer Burns points out in "Essay on Sources" in *Goddess of the Market: Ayn Rand and the American Right* (New York: Oxford University Press, 2009), 291–298, the editor made changes in the text of the

journals that sometimes alter meaning. The section on *The Little Street* can be found in David Harriman, ed., *The Journals of Ayn Rand* (New York: Plume/Penguin Putnam, 1997), 20–48; subsequent quotations are from this source.

4. John Kenneth Galbraith, "Introduction" to Robert Shaplen, *Kreuger, Genius and Swindler* (New York: Alfred A. Knopf, 1960), x.

5. Michael Goodwin, "Introduction" to Darryl Cunningham's graphic novel *The Age of Selfishness: Ayn Rand, Morality, and the Financial Crisis* (New York: Abrams ComicArts, 2015), iv–v.

6. Ayn Rand, *The Romantic Manifesto* (New York: World, 1969; paperback New York: New American Library, 1971). The quoted lines are the opening to essay no. 11, "The Goal of My Writing," 155 (1971 ed.).

7. Ayn Rand's childhood fantasy hero, the fictional hero Cyrus Palton of *The Mysterious Valley*, is discussed in chapter 1.

8. Gary Percesepe, "Ayn Rand and the American Psyche: An Interview with Mary Gaitskill," *Nervous Breakdown*, July 14, 2011. In this interview, novelist Gaitskill talks about reading Rand at age fifteen and then interviewing Rand followers when she was twenty-eight for her novel *Two Girls, Fat and Thin* (New York: Simon & Schuster, 1991). With great insight and sympathy, she describes young Rand converts as "cobbling together" a sense of life and purpose through fantasies imposed on experience.

9. Ayn Rand, "Art and Sense of Life," in *The Romantic Manifesto*, 2nd rev. ed. (1969; New York: New American Library, 1975), 24–25.

10. Raymond Williams, *Marxism and Literature* (London: Oxford University Press, 1977), 133.

11. Lauren Berlant, *Cruel Optimism* (Durham, NC: Duke University Press, 2011), 16.

12. Introduction to Alvin Toffler, "Playboy Interview: Ayn Rand," *Playboy*, Mar. 1964.

13. From Ayn Rand, "Introducing Objectivism," in *The Ayn Rand Lexicon: Objectivism from A to Z*, ed. Harry Binswanger (New York: New American Library, 1988).

14. Quoted in Burns, *Goddess of the Market*, 177n20, 324.

15. Mimi Reisel Gladstein and Chris Matthew Sciabarra, eds., *Feminist Interpretations of Ayn Rand* (University Park: Pennsylvania State University Press, 1999), esp. Melissa Jane Hardie, "Fluff and Granite: Rereading Rand's Camp Feminist Aesthetics," 363–389.

16. See above, note 8.

17. Gabriel Mitchell, "Queer Themes in Ayn Rand," https://gabrieljmitchell.com/2016/11/23/queer-themes-in-ayn-rand.

18. See Chris Matthew Sciabarra, *Ayn Rand, Homosexuality, and Human Liberation* (Cape Town, South Africa: Leap, 2003).

19. On the 2017 Brooklyn Academy of Music production of Ivo van Hove's *The Fountainhead*, see Ben Brantley, "'The Fountainhead,' High Tech, Juicy, and Full of Pulp," *New York Times*, Nov. 29, 2017.

20. Umberto Eco, "*Casablanca:* Cult Movies and Intertextual Collage," *SubStance* 14, no. 2 (1985): 3–12, quoted in Claudia Franziska Brühwiler, "Pitiless Adolescents and Young Crusaders: Reimagining Ayn Rand's Readers," *Canadian Review of American Studies* 46, no. 1 (Spring 2016): 42–61.

CHAPTER ONE. "PROUD WOMAN CONQUEROR"

1. Two relatively recent biographies provide excellent accounts of Ayn Rand's life. One is by historian Jennifer Burns, *Goddess of the Market: Any Rand and the American Right* (New York: Oxford University Press, 2009), and the other by journalist Anne Heller, *Ayn Rand and the World She Made* (New York: Nan Talese/Doubleday, 2009). Burns had access to Ayn Rand Institute archives, usually restricted to scholars sympathetic to Rand's philosophy of Objectivism. She was able to compare the published letters and journals with the originals, as well as to examine interviews and notes not yet published. Her biography is thus authoritative in quotations and details. Heller did not have access to the ARI archives, but she did more basic research on the Russian imperial and Soviet era of Rand's life. Further details are found in an interview with Rand's youngest sister, Eleanora (Nora) Rosenbaum Drobysheva, in Scott McConnell, *100 Voices: An Oral History of Ayn Rand* (New York: New American Library, 2010), 3–19, and in Chris Matthew

Sciabarra, *Ayn Rand: The Russian Radical* (University Park: Pennsylvania State University Press, 1995).

2. There is a discussion of "The Mysterious Valley" and Cyrus Paltons's character, complete with illustration, in Jeff Britting, *Ayn Rand* (New York: Overlook Duckworth, 2004), 7–8.

3. Broad accounts of the history of the Russian empire, both before and during the early Soviet period, are provided in Andreas Kappeler, *The Russian Empire: A Multi-Ethnic History* (London: Pearson Education, 2001); Terry Martin, *The Affirmative Action Empire: Nations and Nationalism in the Soviet Union* (Ithaca, NY: Cornell University Press, 2001); and Liliana Riga, *The Bolsheviks and the Russian Empire* (Cambridge: Cambridge University Press, 2012).

4. See Zvi Gitelman, *A Century of Ambivalence: The Jews of Russia and the Soviet Union, 1881 to the Present* (Bloomington: Indiana University Press, 2000); and Yuri Slezkine, *The Jewish Century* (Princeton, NJ: Princeton University Press, 2005). Liliana Riga also has a very interesting discussion of Jewish leadership among the Bolsheviks in *The Bolsheviks and the Russian Empire*. See also Richard P. Stephens, "Zionism as a Phase of Western Imperialism," in *The Transformation of Palestine*, ed. Ibrahim Abu-Lughod (Evanston, IL: Northwestern University Press, 1971), 27–59.

5. For discussion of ideas about gender and sexuality before and after the revolution, see Wendy Goldman, *Women, the State, and Revolution: Soviet Family Policy and Social Life, 1917–1936* (Cambridge: Cambridge University Press, 1993); Dan Healy, *Homosexual Desire in Revolutionary Russia* (Chicago: University of Chicago Press, 2001); and most provocatively, Eric Naiman, *Sex in Public: The Incarnation of Early Soviet Ideology* (Princeton, NJ: Princeton University Press, 1997).

6. On the revolution, see the mainstream overview in Sheila Fitzpatrick, *The Russian Revolution*, 4th ed. (New York: Oxford University Press, 2017); and the more pointed political analysis in Vijay Prashad, *Red Star over the Third World* (New Delhi: LeftWord Books, 2017).

7. Scott McConnell, "Parallel Lives: Models and Inspirations for Characters in *We the Living*," in *Essays on Ayn Rand's "We the Living,"* 2nd ed., ed. Robert Mayhew (New York: Lexington Books, 2012), 51.

8. On filmmaking in Russia before and after the revolution, see Denise Youngblood, *The Magic Mirror: Moviemaking in Russia, 1908–1918* (Madison: University of Wisconsin Press, 1999); and Denise Youngblood, *Movies for the Masses: Popular Cinema and Soviet Society in the 1920s* (Cambridge: Cambridge University Press, 1992).

9. Ayn Rand, *We the Living* (1959; New York: New American Library, 2009), includes the widely cited quote from Lenin on p. 363. Rand's movie diary is reprinted in Michael Berliner, ed., *Ayn Rand: Russian Writings on Hollywood* (Irvine, CA: Ayn Rand Institute Press, 1999), 115–221. See also Meenakshi Shedde and Vinzenz Hediger, "Come On, Baby, Be My Tiger: Inventing India on the German Screen in *Der Tiger von Eschnapur* and *Das indische Grabmal*," in *Import/Export: Cultural Transfer between India and Germany*, ed. M. Dutta, A. Fitz, M Kroge, A. Schneider, and D. Wenner (Berlin: Parthas, 2005).

10. "Hollywood: American City of Movies," written while Rand was still in Russia, is included in Berliner, *Ayn Rand: Russian Writings on Hollywood*, 43–106.

11. "Pola Negri" is also included in Berliner, *Ayn Rand: Russian Writings in Hollywood*, 15–40.

12. The "Red Pawn" plot summary is reprinted in Leonard Peikoff, ed., *The Early Ayn Rand: A Selection from Her Unpublished Fiction*, rev. ed. (New York: New American Library, 2005), 154–227. See also Jena Trammell, "Red Pawn: Ayn Rand's Other Story of Soviet Russia," in Mayhew, ed., *Essays on Ayn Rand's "We the Living,"* 279–297.

13. Rand, "Foreword," *We the Living*, xii.

14. David Harriman, ed., *Journals of Ayn Rand* (New York: Plume/ Penguin, 1999), 50–51.

15. Rand, *We the Living*, 352–353.

16. Harriman, ed., *Journals of Ayn Rand*, 50–51.

17. Rand, *We the Living*, 45.

18. Ibid.,437–438.

19. Ibid., 53–54.

20. Ibid., 417.

21. Ibid., 158.

22. Ibid., 362–367.

23. See Richard Ralston, "Publishing *We the Living*," and Jeff Britting, "Adapting *We the Living*," both in Mayhew, ed., *Essays on Ayn Rand's "We the Living*," 159–170 and 181–208, respectively.

24. Both Ayn Rand and left anarchist Emma Goldman came to oppose both the Bolsheviks and the European fascists, but from opposite ends of the political spectrum. Comparison of *We the Living* to Emma Goldman, *My Disillusionment in Russia* (Garden City, NY: Doubleday, Page, 1924), is revelatory.

25. Hoberman quoted in Michael S. Berliner, "Reviews of *We the Living*," in Mayhew, ed., *Essays on Ayn Rand's "We the Living*," 179.

CHAPTER TWO. "INDIVIDUALISTS OF THE
WORLD UNITE!"

1. See chapter 1, note 1, for sources of biographical details.

2. For accounts of the political economy of Hollywood, see Douglas Gomery, *The Hollywood Studio System: A History* (London: British Film Institute, 2005), and especially the excellent and ambitious book by Lee Grieveson, *Cinema and the Wealth of Nations* (Oakland: University of California Press, 2018).

3. See Michael Paul Rogin, *Blackface, White Noise: Jewish Immigrants in the Hollywood Melting Pot* (Berkeley: University of California Press, 1996); Neal Gabler, *An Empire of Their Own: How the Jews Invented Hollywood* (New York: Random House, 1988); and especially Cedric Robinson, *Forgeries of Memory and Meaning: Blacks and the Regimes of Race in American Theater and Film before World War II* (Chapel Hill: University of North Carolina Press, 2007), chapter 2, "In the Year 1915: D. W. Griffith and the Rewhitening of America," 82–126.

4. For a good biography of DeMille, see Sumiko Higashi, *Cecil B. DeMille and American Culture: The Silent Era* (Berkeley: University of California Press, 1994).

5. Billed by its publisher as "The Classic Work on Communism in America during the Thirties," Eugene Lyons's *The Red Decade* (New York: Arlington House, 1941) lays out the hyperventilating paranoia about the Reds infiltrating American culture and politics in the

thirties that influenced Rand. In his future role as an editor at *Reader's Digest,* Lyons published Rand's own anticommunist screed "The Only Path to Tomorrow" in the January 1944 issue (88–90).

6. "The Individualist Manifesto" was never published. The typescript in the Ayn Rand Archives is quoted and discussed by Jennifer Burns, *Goddess of the Market: Ayn Rand and the American Right* (New York: Oxford University Press, 2009), 61–66. "The Only Path to Tomorrow," cited above, is a condensed version of the "Manifesto."

7. See Jim Powell, "Rose Wilder Lane, Isabel Paterson, and Ayn Rand: The Women Who Inspired the Modern Libertarian Movement," *Foundation for Economic Education,* May 1, 1986; Judith Thurman, "A Libertarian House on the Prairie," *New Yorker,* Aug. 16, 2012; and Jennifer Burns, "The Three Furies of Libertarianism: Rose Wilder Lane, Isabel Paterson, and Ayn Rand," *Journal of American History* 102, no. 3 (Dec. 2015): 746–774.

8. For the summary of Rand's "Screen Guide for Americans," see Thomas F. Brady, "Hollywood Don'ts," *New York Times,* Nov. 16, 1947, X5.

9. The dilemma of the Hollywood moguls is extensively described in Gabler, *An Empire of Their Own,* and in Grieveson, *Cinema and the Wealth of Nations,* chapter 13, "The World of Tomorrow—Today!," 313–335.

10. Ayn Rand, *Anthem* (1938; [Lexington, KY]: Mockingbird Classics, 2015), 42–43.

11. Yevgeny Zamyatin, *We* (New York: E.P. Dutton, 1924); Aldous Huxley, *Brave New World* (London: Chatto & Windus, 1932).

12. Scott McConnell, *100 Voices: An Oral History of Ayn Rand* (New York: New American Library, 2010), 492, 496–497.

13. Before *Anthem, We the Living* and *Red Pawn* featured romantic triangles, but they were not ferociously eroticized like those in *The Fountainhead* and *Atlas Shrugged.*

14. Rand's relationship with Isabel Paterson is discussed in Burns, *Goddess of the Market,* 74–78, 125–129, and in Anne Heller, *Ayn Rand and the World She Made* (New York: Doubleday, 2009), 135–137.

15. An exegesis of the unpublished typescript of "The Individualist Manifesto" is included in Burns, *Goddess of the Market,* 61–66.

16. Ayn Rand, *The Fountainhead* (1943; New York: Signet/New American Library, 1952), 15–16.

17. David Harriman, ed., *The Journals of Ayn Rand* (New York: Plume/Penguin Putnam, 1997), 93.

18. Ibid., 97.

19. Ibid., 102.

20. Ayn Rand, *The Fountainhead*, 111.

21. Susan Brownmiller, "Ayn Rand: A Traitor to Her Sex," in *Feminist Interpretations of Ayn Rand*, ed. Mimi Gladstein and Chris Sciabarra (University Park: Pennsylvania State University Press, 1999), 63–65.

22. Ayn Rand, *The Fountainhead*, 216–218

23. Harriman, ed., *Journals of Ayn Rand*, 230–231.

24. Eve Kosofsky Sedgwick, *Between Men: English Literature and Male Homosocial Desire* (New York: Columbia University Press, 1985).

25. Harriman, ed., *Journals of Ayn Rand*, 233.

26. Rand was not a close reader of Nietzsche, but more of a fan, until she eschewed his influence during the writing of *The Fountainhead*. In her introduction to the twenty-fifth-anniversary edition of that novel (x), she calls him a "mystic" and an "irrationalist" and says she removed quotations from his work at the heading of each manuscript chapter before the book was published.

27. Orville Prescott, Review of *The Fountainhead, New York Times*, May 12, 1943, 23.

28. Lorine Pruette, "Battle against Evil: *The Fountainhead*, by Ayn Rand," *New York Times Book Review*, May 16, 1943, 7.

29. For a discussion of metaphors of revelation and awakening in Ayn Rand's fan mail, and of her own commitment to appeal to feeling in her novels, see Burns, *Goddess of the Market*, 91–93. Michael Berliner discusses the full range of reviews in "*The Fountainhead* Reviews," in *Essays on Ayn Rand's "The Fountainhead,"* ed. Robert Mayhew (Lanham, MD: Lexington Books, 2007), 77–85.

30. Linda Williams, *Playing the Race Card: Melodramas of Black and White from Uncle Tom to O. J. Simpson* (Princeton, NJ: Princeton University Press, 2001), 192–194, discusses *Uncle Tom's Cabin* and *Gone with the Wind* as "trans genre media events." *The Fountainhead* has many

resemblances to *Gone with the Wind.* For a discussion of the making of the movie *The Fountainhead,* see Matthew Harle, "Trump at the Movies: Dismantling Ayn Rand's *The Fountainhead,*" *Cineaste,* Summer 2017, 10–17. On King Vidor's hands-off approach to directing *The Fountainhead,* see Raymond Durgnat and Scott Simon, *King Vidor, American* (Berkeley: University of California Press, 1988), 257–269.

31. See Grieveson, *Cinema and the Wealth of Nations,* 313–335.

32. Corey Robin, *The Reactionary Mind,* 2nd ed. (New York: Oxford University Press, 2018).

CHAPTER THREE. "WOULD YOU CUT THE BIBLE?"

1. See Kim Phillips-Fein, *Invisible Hands: The Making of the Conservative Movement from the New Deal to Reagan* (New York: W.W. Norton, 2009), and Brian Doherty, *Radicals for Capitalism: A Freewheeling History of the Modern American Libertarian Movement* (New York: Public Affairs/Perseus Books, 2007).

2. William F. Buckley, *Getting It Right* (New York: Regnery Publishing, 2003).

3. Nora Ephron, in "A Strange Kind of Simplicity," *New York Times,* May 5, 1968, suggested that the name Branden was concocted from the Hebrew for "son of Rand," or ben Rand.

4. Quoted in Nathaniel Branden, *Judgment Day: My Years with Ayn Rand,* rev. ed. (1989; New York: Houghton Mifflin, 1999), chap. 10.

5. For a summary of the various reviews, see Michael Berliner, "The *Atlas Shrugged* Reviews," in *Essays on Ayn Rand's "Atlas Shrugged,"* ed. Robert Mayhew (Lanham, MD: Lexington Books, 2009).

6. Granville Hicks, "A Parable of Buried Talents," *New York Times,* Oct. 13, 1957.

7. Whittaker Chambers, "Big Sister Is Watching You," *National Review,* Jan. 5, 2005.

8. Ruth Alexander in the *New York Daily Mirror,* quoted in Barbara Branden, *The Passion of Ayn Rand* (New York: Doubleday, 1986), 298.

9. Ludwig von Mises to Ayn Rand, Jan. 23, 1958, at https://mises .org/library/ludwig-von-misess-letter-rand-atlas-shrugged.

10. "The Solid-Gold Dollar Sign," *Time,* Oct. 14, 1957.

11. Berliner, *"Atlas Shrugged* Reviews," 134. Berliner notes that Ayn Rand's files contain clippings of hundreds of reviews of *Atlas Shrugged,* but only fourteen are positive.

12. Such terms appear often in Ayn Rand's journals; see, e.g., David Harriman, ed., *The Journals of Ayn Rand* (New York: Plume/Penguin, 1999), 489–652.

13. Ayn Rand, *Atlas Shrugged* (New York: Random House, 1957), 664.

14. Bennett Cerf's version of this encounter is presented in Anne Heller, *Ayn Rand and the World She Made* (New York: Doubleday, 2009), 279.

15. Numerous critical accounts of bureaucratic organizational life were published during the 1950s, including David Riesman, Nathan Glazer, and Reuel Denney, *The Lonely Crowd* (New Haven, CT: Yale University Press, 1950); William H. Whyte Jr., *The Organization Man* (New York: Simon & Schuster, 1956); and Sloan Wilson, *The Man in the Gray Flannel Suit* (New York: Simon & Schuster, 1955).

16. Judith Wilt, "On *Atlas Shrugged,*" in *Feminist Interpretations of Ayn Rand,* ed. Mimi Reisel Gladstein and Chris Matthew Sciabarra (University Park: Pennsylvania State University Press, 1999), 57–65.

17. Melissa Jane Hardie, "Fluff and Granite: Rereading Rand's Camp Feminist Aesthetics," in Gladstein and Sciabarra, eds., *Feminist Interpretations of Ayn Rand,* 363–386.

18. Jennifer Burns, *Goddess of the Market: Ayn Rand and the American Right* (New York: Oxford University Press, 2009), 181.

19. Nathaniel Branden and Barbara Branden, *Who Is Ayn Rand?* (New York: Random House, 1962).

20. "Born Eccentric," *Newsweek,* Mar. 27, 1961; John Kobler, "The Curious Cult of Ayn Rand," *Saturday Evening Post,* Nov. 11, 1961.

21. Murray Rothbard, "The Sociology of the Ayn Rand Cult," cited in Burns, *Goddess of the Market,* 184.

22. Albert Ellis quoted in Heller, *Ayn Rand and the World She Made,* 364.

23. N. Branden, *Judgment Day,* 226.

24. Ayn Rand's lecture "Faith and Force: The Destroyers of the Modern World" was published in Ayn Rand, *Philosophy: Who Needs It* (New York: Signet/New American Library, 1984), 58–75.

25. Quoted in Heller, *Ayn Rand and the World She Made,* 309.

26. Alvin Toffler, "Playboy Interview: Ayn Rand," *Playboy,* Mar. 1964.

27. See Barry Goldwater, *The Conscience of a Conservative* (Shepardsville, KY: Victor, 1960) (ghostwritten by William F. Buckley Jr.'s son-in-law L. Brent Bozell), and Rick Perlstein, *Before the Storm: Barry Goldwater and the Unmaking of the American Consensus* (New York: Nation Books, 2009).

28. Roy Childs Papers, Box 31, "Objectivism—Ayn Rand," Hoover Institute Archives, Stanford University; cited in Burns, *Goddess of the Market,* 335n67.

29. N. Branden, *Judgment Day,* chap. 17.

30. Jerome Tuccille argues that Objectivism appealed especially to young Jews and Catholics from the middle classes; see *It Usually Begins with Ayn Rand* (New York: Stein & Day, 1971), 10.

31. Examples of Rand's clear public lectures include "Philosophy: Who Needs It" and "Faith and Force: The Destroyers of the Modern World," both in Rand, *Philosophy: Who Needs It,* 1–11 and 58–75, respectively.

32. The full transcript of Mike Wallace's interview with Rand is available at http://glamour-and-discourse.blogspot.com/p/mike-wallace-interviews-ayn-rand.html.

33. Tuccille, *It Usually Begins with Ayn Rand,* 11.

34. Ayn Rand, *For the New Intellectual: The Philosophy of Ayn Rand* (New York: Signet/New American Library, 1961).

35. Gore Vidal, "Comment," *Esquire,* July 1961.

36. "Racism" is essay no. 17 in Ayn Rand and Nathaniel Branden, *The Virtue of Selfishness: A New Concept of Egoism* (New York: New American Library, 1961).

37. Ayn Rand, "The Wreckage of the Consensus," in *Capitalism: The Unknown Ideal* (New York: Signet/New American Library, 1966), 249–266.

38. Ayn Rand, "The Age of Envy," in *The New Left: The Anti-Industrial Revolution* (New York: New American Library, 1971), 130–158.

CHAPTER FOUR. "I FOUND A FLAW"

1. Douglas Rushkoff, "Survival of the Richest: The Wealthy Are Plotting to Leave Us Behind," *Medium*, July 5, 2018.

2. Stan Lehr and Louis Rossetto, Jr., "The New Right Credo—Libertarianism," *New York Times Magazine*, Jan. 10, 1971.

3. Quoted in Jennifer Burns, *Goddess of the Market: Ayn Rand and the American Right* (New York: Oxford University Press, 2009), 258.

4. David Kelley split from the "official" Objectivist Ayn Rand Institute to found the Institute for Objectivist Studies in 1990. Renamed the Atlas Society in 2006, Kelley's group considers Rand's work as a flexible framework, in dialogue with other philosophies, rather than as a rigid orthodoxy. There is also a tiny Objectivist Party, founded in 2008, as well as other organizations and individuals who follow Rand without adhering to the ARI line.

5. See Philip Mirowski and Dieter Plehwe, *The Road from Mont Pelerin: The Making of a Neoliberal Thought Collective* (Cambridge, MA: Harvard University Press, 2009). Mirowski expands this analysis in *Never Let a Serious Crisis Go to Waste* (New York: Verso Books, 2013).

6. In *Globalists: The End of Empire and the Birth of Neoliberalism* (Cambridge, MA: Harvard University Press, 2018), Neil Slobodian argues that neoliberals did not shrink the state; they redeployed it.

7. David Harvey, *A Brief History of Neoliberalism* (New York: Oxford University Pres, 2005).

8. See Nancy MacLean, *Democracy in Chains: The Deep History of the Radical Right's Stealth Plan for America* (New York: Viking, 2017); and Ronald Radosh, "Steve Bannon, Trump's Top Guy, Told Me He Was 'a Leninist,'" *Daily Beast*, Aug. 22, 2016.

9. Nancy MacLean develops the idea of "property supremacy" in *Democracy in Chains*.

10. For an account of the rise of right-wing populism after the 2008 economic meltdown, see Federico Finchelstein, *From Fascism to Populism in History* (Oakland: University of California Press, 2017); and Paolo Gerbaudo, *The Mask and the Flag: Populism, Citizenship, and Global Protest* (New York: Oxford University Press, 2017).

11. For discussions of everyday neoliberalism and the construction of neoliberal modes of being, see Philip Mirowski, *Never Let a Serious Crisis Go to Waste,* and Wendy Brown, *Undoing the Demos: Neoliberalism's Stealth Revolution* (Cambridge, MA: Zone Books/MIT Press, 2015). For another view, outlining the relationship of neoliberalism and issues of disability/capacity, see Robert McRuer, *Crip Times: Disability, Globalization, and Resistance* (New York: NYU Press, 2018).

12. Mirowski, *Never Let a Serious Crisis Go to Waste,* 129.

13. For an analysis of neoliberalism as a story, see Fredric Jameson, *Representing "Capital": A Reading of Volume One* (New York: Verso Books, 2011).

14. Alan Greenspan, *The Age of Turbulence: Adventures in a New World* (New York: Penguin, 2007), 53.

15. See Sebastian Mallaby, *The Man Who Knew Too Much: The Life and Times of Alan Greenspan* (New York: Penguin, 2016).

16. Nick Bilton, "Silicon Valley's Most Disturbing Obsession," *Vanity Fair,* Oct. 5, 2016.

17. Greenspan has been quoted saying various permutations of "I found a flaw" or "I've found a flaw" or "I discovered a flaw." For the first version, see "Greenspan Admits 'Flaw' in Ideology," *Aljazeera,* Oct. 26, 2008.

18. Ed Kilgore, "Donald Trump's Role Model Is an Ayn Rand Character," *Intelligencer,* Apr. 12, 2016.

19. See, e.g., Robert Reich, "Trump's Brand Is Ayn Rand," *Nation of Change,* Mar. 6, 2018.

20. There is currently much speculation about whether neoliberalism is collapsing. For a compelling argument that it has already collapsed and been replaced by security states in the Global South, see Paul Amar, *The Security Archipelago: Human-Security States, Sexuality Politics, and the End of Neoliberalism* (Durham, NC: Duke University Press, 2013).

GLOSSARY

BOLSHEVIK REVOLUTION The October 1917 Russian revolution that overthrew the czarist regime, installed an embattled socialist government, and profoundly influenced Ayn Rand's political views.

CAPITALISM The political, economic, social, and cultural organization of life based on private property and the profit motive. Emerging during the fifteenth to seventeenth centuries in Europe, capitalism came to dominate the global economy. Ayn Rand justified and glorified the forms of human inequality that are central to the history of capitalism.

CIVILIZATIONAL DISCOURSE The interrelated advocacy of economic domination and racial hierarchy that supported European imperial expansion. Capitalism, Christianity, and white supremacy are linked as achievements that develop through progress over time. Ayn Rand invoked civilizational discourse in her fiction and nonfiction.

FASCISM A form of authoritarian nationalism that rose to prominence in early and mid-twentieth-century Europe. Fascists advocated state-controlled capitalism, based in the inequalities established through civilizational discourse. Ayn Rand advocated laissez-faire capitalism and opposed fascism.

107

IMPERIALISM The process of extending the control of territorial political economies over other regions, by military force, administrative control, and/or economic and cultural domination. Ayn Rand admired European imperial culture and American imperial aspirations.

LIBERTARIANISM Advocacy of individual, social, political, and economic freedom from state control. Different forms of libertarianism exist across the political spectrum, overlapping with anarchist communism as well as "pure" unregulated capitalism. Ayn Rand is an icon of right-wing libertarianism, but she rejected the label during her lifetime.

NATHANIEL BRANDEN INSTITUTE Founded by Rand acolyte Nathaniel Branden as the Nathaniel Branden Lectures in 1958, NBI was dedicated to disseminating the views of Ayn Rand and her philosophy of Objectivism. NBI sponsored courses, distributed tape recordings, printed materials, and sponsored social activities for Objectivists until it disbanded in 1968.

NEOLIBERALISM An ideological and policy model that developed from the 1940s in the United States and Europe and came to dominate the global economy by the 1980s. Often mischaracterized as the reemergence of laissez-faire capitalist advocacy of a minimal state, neoliberal policies actually reconfigured powerful security states to redistribute resources upward and reinvented modes of colonial extraction for the neo/postcolonial period.

OBJECTIVISM The philosophy of Ayn Rand, outlined in her nonfiction writing and advocated through organizations including the Nathaniel Branden Institute, the Ayn Rand Institute, and the Atlas Society. Objectivists advocate capitalism and adhere to a heroic view of striving individuals, dedicated to their own happiness, as the moral foundation for human life.

SENSE OF LIFE Ayn Rand's conception of the overall set of thoughts and feelings that shape and motivate an individual's life, prior to the development of a clear rational plan for living.

KEY FIGURES

NATHANIEL AND BARBARA BRANDEN Born Nathan Blumenthal and
Barbara Weidman, the Brandens married in 1951 and became Ayn
Rand's primary acolytes, a status that lasted until 1968 when a
major split over Nathaniel's affair with Rand sundered organized
Objectivism. They divorced, and Nathaniel Branden, a
psychologist, became a founder of the California self-esteem
movement. Both authored memoirs of their time with Rand.
Barbara Branden's book became a motion picture starring
Helen Mirren.

WILLIAM BUCKLEY Major conservative commentator and founder of the
National Review, Buckley was a vociferous critic of Ayn Rand's atheist
brand of laissez-faire capitalism. His novel *Getting It Right* (2003)
featured Rand as a character defeated and sidelined by history.

WHITTAKER CHAMBERS Chambers was a member of the Communist
Party and a Soviet spy who converted to conservative
anticommunism during the 1950s. He wrote the most
notoriously stinging review of Ayn Rand's *Atlas Shrugged* in
the *National Review* in 1957.

CECILE B. DEMILLE A Hollywood-based producer/director during the
early twentieth century, DeMille is considered a founder of the

popular cinema of the United States. He directed seventy features both silent and sound, and he gave Ayn Rand her first jobs in Hollywood—first as an extra on a film and then as a script reader for his studio.

ALAN GREENSPAN An American economist who was a member of Ayn Rand's "Collective," or inner circle, during the 1950s, Greenspan served as chair of the Federal Reserve from 1987 to 2006. He advocated the deregulation of financial institutions, a policy that is widely viewed as responsible for the 2007–2008 economic crash.

FRIEDRICH HAYEK An Austrian-British economist and philosopher, Hayek was a core member of the Austrian School of economics and a founder of the Mont Pelerin Society. He was at the center of the development of neoliberal policy ideas.

FRIEDRICH NIETZSCHE The work of German philosopher Nietzsche has exerted a profound influence on Western intellectual history. Ayn Rand initially admired his critique of religion and Christian morality, and his concept of the "Superman," but she later repudiated him as a mystic and foe of her brand of rationalism.

FRANK O'CONNOR Ayn Rand met the exquisitely conventionally handsome O'Connor when both were working as extras on a Cecil B. DeMille film set. They married in 1929, which allowed Rand to apply for U.S. citizenship. O'Connor later worked as a florist, pursued training as a painter, and ultimately became a withdrawn alcoholic.

ISABEL PATTERSON A Canadian American journalist, novelist, and political philosopher, Patterson was Ayn Rand's only true mentor and friend during the 1940s in New York City. Her philosophical work *God of the Machine* was published the same year as Rand's *The Fountainhead*. They had a falling-out in the late 1940s.

LEONARD PEIKOFF A Canadian American Objectivist philosopher, Peikoff became a follower of Rand during the 1950s. When most other members of her close circles split from Rand, Peikoff remained fiercely loyal. He became her heir, executor, and founder of the Ayn Rand Institute in 1985.

LUDWIG VON MISES Mises, an Austrian American economist of the Austrian School, is considered a founder of neoliberalism. He wrote Ayn Rand a fan letter in 1958 and invited her to attend his seminar at New York University.

SELECTED BIBLIOGRAPHY

Mean Girl is not a biography of Ayn Rand, nor is it a social history. The biographical sections of the chapters are not based on original research but rely on Barbara Branden's "A Biographical Essay" in Barbara and Nathaniel Branden, *Who is Ayn Rand?* (1962), based on extensive interviews with Rand, as well as on Barbara Branden's updated version in *The Passion of Ayn Rand* (1986). Biographical details are also drawn from the publications of numerous Objectivist scholars admitted to the Ayn Rand Archives (outsiders and critics are usually denied access) and on Chris Sciabarra's *Ayn Rand: The Russian Radical* (1995). But the biographical sketches in *Mean Girl* rely most substantially on the two major 2009 biographies of Rand by Jennifer Burns, *Goddess of the Market: Ayn Rand and the American Right,* and Anne Heller, *Ayn Rand and the World She Made.* The biographical discussions are included to illuminate the historical context and impact of the publication and circulation of Ayn Rand's two major novels, *The Fountainhead* and *Atlas Shrugged. Mean Girl* does not offer close readings of those novels in the manner of a literary critic, however. The novels are considered as treatises, presented in fictional narrative form. Read in this way they become vital polemical texts in the rise of the culture of neoliberal greed. The biographical, historical, and fictional are interwoven in a manner unlike the approach of a biographer, historian, or literary critic, but rather in the mode of interdisciplinary American cultural studies.

BOOKS, ARTICLES, AND INTERVIEWS BY AYN RAND

Berliner, Michael, ed. *Ayn Rand: Russian Writings on Hollywood*. Irvine, CA: Ayn Rand Institute Press, 1999.

Harriman, David, ed. *The Journals of Ayn Rand*. New York: Plume/Penguin Putnam, 1997.

Peikoff, Leonard, ed. *The Early Ayn Rand: A Selection from Her Unpublished Fiction*. Rev. ed. New York: New American Library, 2005.

Rand, Ayn. *Anthem*. 1938; [Lexington, KY]: Mockingbird Classics, 2015.

———. *Atlas Shrugged*. New York: Random House, 1957.

———. *Capitalism: The Unknown Ideal*. New York: Signet/New American Library, 1966.

———. *For the New Intellectual: The Philosophy of Ayn Rand*. New York: Signet/New American Library, 1961.

———. *The Fountainhead*. 1943; New York: Signet/New American Library, 1952.

———. *The New Left: The Anti-Industrial Revolution*. New York: New American Library, 1971.

———. *Philosophy: Who Needs It*. New York: Signet/New American Library, 1984.

———. *The Romantic Manifesto*. New York: World, 1969; paperback New York: New American Library, 1971.

———. *We the Living*. 1959; New York: New American Library, 2009.

Rand, Ayn, and Nathaniel Branden. *The Virtue of Selfishness: A New Concept of Egoism*. New York: New American Library, 1961.

Toffler, Alvin. "Playboy Interview: Ayn Rand." *Playboy*, Mar. 1964.

BOOKS AND ARTICLES ON AYN RAND

Binswanger, Harry, ed. *The Ayn Rand Lexicon: Objectivism from A to Z*. New York: New American Library, 1988.

Branden, Barbara. *The Passion of Ayn Rand.* New York: Doubleday, 1986.

Branden, Nathaniel. *Judgment Day: My Years with Ayn Rand.* New York: Houghton Mifflin, 1989; rev. ed. 1999.

Branden, Nathaniel, and Barbara Branden. *Who Is Ayn Rand?* New York: Random House, 1962.

Britting, Jeff. *Ayn Rand.* New York: Overlook Duckworth, 2004.

Buckley, William. *Getting It Right.* New York: Regnery Publishing, 2003.

Burns, Jennifer. *Goddess of the Market: Ayn Rand and the American Right.* New York: Oxford University Press, 2009.

———. "The Three Furies of Libertarianism: Rose Wilder Lane, Isabel Paterson, and Ayn Rand." *Journal of American History* 102, no. 3 (Dec. 2015): 746–774.

Cunningham, Daryl. *The Age of Selfishness: Ayn Rand, Morality, and the Financial Crisis.* New York: Abrams ComicArts, 2015.

Ephron, Nora. "A Strange Kind of Simplicity." *New York Times,* May 5, 1968.

Gladstein, Mimi Reisl, and Chris Matthew Sciabarra, eds. *Feminist Interpretations of Ayn Rand.* University Park: Pennsylvania State University Press, 1999.

Greenspan, Alan. *The Age of Turbulence: Adventures in a New World.* New York: Penguin Press, 2007.

Heller, Anne. *Ayn Rand and the World She Made.* New York: Nan Talese/Doubleday, 2009.

Mayhew, Robert, ed. *Essays on Ayn Rand's "Atlas Shrugged."* Lanham, MD: Lexington Books, 2009.

———, ed. *Essays on Ayn Rand's "The Fountainhead."* Lanham, MD: Lexington Books, 2007.

———, ed. *Essays on Ayn Rand's "We the Living."* 2nd ed. New York: Lexington Books, 2012.

McConnell, Scott. *100 Voices: An Oral History of Ayn Rand.* New York: New American Library, 2010.

Sciabarra, Chris Matthew. *Ayn Rand, Homosexuality, and Human Liberation.* Cape Town, South Africa: Leap, 2003.

———. *Ayn Rand: The Russian Radical.* University Park: Pennsylvania State University Press, 1995.

Tuccille, Jerome. *It Usually Begins with Ayn Rand.* New York: Stein & Day, 1971.

Turner, Jenny. "As Astonishing as Elvis." *London Review of Books,* Dec. 1, 2005.

Žižek, Slavoj. "The Actuality of Ayn Rand." *Journal of Ayn Rand Studies* 3, no. 2 (2002): 215–227.

BOOKS ON GREED AND NEOLIBERAL CAPITALISM

Amar, Paul. *The Security Archipelago: Human-Security States, Sexuality Politics, and the End of Neoliberalism.* Durham, NC: Duke University Press, 2013.

Berlant, Lauren. *Cruel Optimism.* Durham, NC: Duke University Press, 2011.

Doherty, Brian. *Radicals for Capitalism: A Freewheeling History of the Modern American Libertarian Movement.* New York: Public Affairs/Perseus Books, 2007.

Harvey, David. *A Brief History of Neoliberalism.* New York: Oxford University Press, 2005.

MacLean, Nancy. *Democracy in Chains: The Deep History of the Radical Right's Stealth Plan for America.* New York: Viking, 2017.

Mirowski, Philip. *Never Let a Serious Crisis Go to Waste.* New York: Verso Books, 2013.

Mirowski, Philip, and Dieter Plehwe. *The Road from Mont Pelerin: The Making of a Neoliberal Thought Collective.* Cambridge, MA: Harvard University Press, 2009.

Phillips-Fein, Kim. *Invisible Hands: The Making of the Conservative Movement from the New Deal to Reagan.* New York: W. W. Norton, 2009.

Slobodian, Quinn. *Globalists: The End of Empire and the Birth of Neoliberalism.* Cambridge, MA: Harvard University Press, 2018.